COMMUNITY MEMORIES

Farmers Bank
& Capital Trust Co.
www.farmersfrankfort.com

CELEBRATING 150 YEARS

THIS PUBLICATION WAS MADE POSSIBLE

THROUGH SUPPORT FROM

THE FARMERS BANK & CAPITAL TRUST COMPANY OF

FRANKFORT, KENTUCKY

COMMUNITY MEMORIES

A Glimpse of African American Life in Frankfort, Kentucky

Winona L. Fletcher, *Senior Editor*

Sheila Mason Burton, *Associate Editor*

James E. Wallace, *Associate Editor*

Mary E. Winter, *Photographs Editor*

Douglas A. Boyd, *Oral History Editor*

John Hardin, *Consultant*

with a preface by
GEORGE C. WOLFE

The Kentucky Historical Society

FRANKFORT, KENTUCKY / 2003

© 2003 by The Kentucky Historical Society

Distributed for The Kentucky Historical Society by The University Press of Kentucky

Library of Congress Cataloging-in-Publication Data

Fletcher, Winona L.
    Community memories: a glimpse of African American life in Frankfort, Kentucky /
Winona L. Fletcher, senior editor; Sheila Mason Burton, associate editor; James E.
Wallace, associate editor; Mary E. Winter, photographs editor; Douglas A. Boyd, oral
history editor; John Hardin, consultant.
        p. cm.
    Includes index.
    ISBN 0-916968-30-8 (alk. paper)
        1. African Americans—Kentucky—Frankfort—History. 2. African Americans—
Kentucky—Frankfort—Social Conditions. 3. African Americans—Kentucky—
Frankfort—Interviews. 4. Frankfort (Ky.)—History. 5. Frankfort (Ky.)—Social
conditions. 6. Frankfort (Ky.)—Biography. I. Burton, Sheila Mason, 1948–
II. Wallace, James E., 1957– III. Winter, Mary E., 1953– IV. Boyd, Douglas A., 1970–
V. Kentucky Historical Society. VI. Title.

F459.F8F56 2003
976.9'432—dc21   2002043329

"There are those whose inner selves are afire with purpose and who speak a language which the hearts and ears of others understand and answer."

Dr. Charles Wesley, Historian

Dr. Henry E. Cheaney, pictured with his wife Ora Mae, receives an honorary doctorate from Berea College.

Contributed by Ora Mae Cheaney

This book is dedicated to two unforgettable citizens, Dr. Henry Ellis Cheaney and his wife Ora Mae Williams Cheaney. Transplants from western Kentucky during the Great Depression of the 1930s, they have become synonymous with Kentucky State University, Mayo-Underwood High School, and the city of Frankfort. Together they embody the perfect blend of "town and gown." Loved for their concern and presence at personal family times of joy and sorrow and known as perennial sources of wisdom to all of us, the Cheaneys have received accolades, honors, awards, and admiration in innumerable ways over the years. We humbly add our voices to the throngs of other voices with genuine respect and love.

CONTENTS

FOREWORD

"BORN, BRED AND WED HERE, TWO LIVING ANCESTORS SPEAK"

Mary Ellis and Millie Combs

Publication of this treasured volume of Black Frankfort is an exciting event in the new millennium. As the oldest living city residents whose memories are recorded here, we are proud to be part of this book. Born in 1902, we are witnesses of the progression of human beings and events that span the entire twentieth century. Furthermore, we carry in our heads and hearts memories and facts passed on to us from the nineteenth century by our ancestors, the Traceys and Carters. Very few can claim over 95 years' living in Frankfort. Each of us was born, bred, and wed in this fair city. We stayed here to raise our families and to watch the numbers grow and grow. We are proud of how tightly knit they have remained over the years. How happy we are of this effort to honor and document our presence in the neighborhoods represented on the pages that follow.

We give thanks for this chance to brush the cobwebs from such treasured memories as using the church as our one-room schoolhouse and of hiding our old victrola in the nearby woods until church meetings let out so that we could return to the all-purpose building and start dancing. Some of us never stopped dancing! Or on another level, it warms our hearts to recall a father who would stay up all Saturday night to keep a fire in the wood stove just so the children could be warm next day in Sunday school. Of course, our memories run the whole gamut of the Frankfort experience expressed in this book—births and deaths, joys and sorrows, growth and losses, floods and floodwalls, changes for the best, and changes for the worst.

Needless to say, some of our latent fears have also been brought to the surface by the images shown here. We feel such horror for the evils that have beset our children. Our children are our future, but we know that change must start with the parents if we hope to control the violence and crime and the lack of self-respect and respect for others that fill our streets and homes these days. We yearn for the return of selflessness and caring about others. Why have we forgotten that all of us have something to give others even though we may seem to have only a little bit ourselves? As elders, we are trying to adjust to the changes that come with time or to accept those we cannot change with a sense of humor. Most of all, we thank God for giving us long lives and ask His blessing on the people whose efforts are seen here.

Mary E. Ellis and Millie Combs at the *Community Memories* exhibit in the Old State Capitol, 1995.

Contributed by Winona L. Fletcher

"I never thought I'd be here over 95 years; things like that never dawned on me, you know, like just one day at a time…trying to do something worthwhile."

MARY E. ELLIS
(June 28, 1902 – October 24, 2000)

"I can't do all this old stuff like we used to do 'cause they ain't nobody to do it with me."

MILLIE COMBS
(March 4, 1902 – July 30, 2002)

Sadly, before this manuscript could be published,
both Mrs. Ellis and Mrs. Combs died.

PREFACE

At various times in my career, like standing in front of the Royal Court Theatre in London on the opening night of my play, or in the middle of technical rehearsals for my first Broadway show, when scenery and tempers were about to combust, I remember quite vividly saying to myself, "How did this skinny Negro boy from Frankfort, Kentucky, end up here?"

It was the stakes of the situation, the seeming incongruity of Frankfort, Kentucky, and opening night in London, of skinny Negro Boy and big Broadway musical, which led me to ask the question. For as far as my memory would afford me, one day I was sitting on my Grandmother's front porch at dusk playing "I see something you don't see," or I was in a school closing play at Rosenwald Laboratory School, or playing the trumpet badly at First Baptist Church, the congregation nodding and saying, "Good job," and the next thing I know, I'm in the middle of my career, confronting impossible obstacles and overwhelming possibilities. And so how did this skinny Negro boy from Frankfort, Kentucky, get here? As is frequently the case, the question and the answer are one and the same. I am where I am precisely because of who I am and where I am from.

I am so grateful to be born when and where I was born, surrounded by a community of people, each of whom I felt had a vested, personal investment in my feeling safe and proud in the world, not because I was special, but because I was one of them. The confidence with which I have gone into worlds unknown and asserted my right to be there is in direct relationship to my growing up in a town where my heart, mind, and spirit were fed strong doses of self-worth and permission to believe in my own sense of magic.

In looking at the photographs and reading the accompanying text and interviews in *Community Memories: A Glimpse of African American Life in Frankfort, Kentucky*, I felt this profound sense of home, caring, laughter, and love rush over me. Though certain vestiges of what was Frankfort's Black community are no more (the house where I spent the first ten years of my life on Blanton Street has been devoured by some gargantuan state building), the visceral memory of what that community was and is, lives on. It lives on, not just in the images and words of *Community Memories*, but in the spirits and accomplishments, both large and small, of all who were touched, fed, and flourished inside of the all-encompassing heart of the Black/Negro/Colored/African American community of Frankfort. *Community Memories* is a wonderful document. Read, experience, and enjoy.

GEORGE C. WOLFE,
New York City

George C. Wolfe is a
playwright, producer,
director, and Tony
Award winner,
who now resides in
New York City.
Photo by Julia Maloof

ACKNOWLEDGMENTS

On my retirement from Indiana University in 1994, I returned to Frankfort and volunteered to assist the Community Memories Project with its collection of oral history interviews. I had no idea that I would subsequently inherit the title of senior editor. I accepted the responsibility—reluctantly— when I realized that with a bit of modification the now-familiar African proverb, "it takes a village to raise a child," was really what this book was about. *It was going to take a village to prepare this book.* Many hands did not always make light work, as the saying goes, but knowing they were always there certainly lifted my spirit. And so, for the many hands, hearts, and minds that made this publication possible, I give thanks.

I acknowledge gratitude to the forces and people behind the "idea" of this book: Historic Frankfort, Inc., the Kentucky Historical Society, and African American citizens who came forward to serve. I especially acknowledge the contributions of Sheila Mason Burton, Barbara White, Dorothy McGowan, John Sykes, Brooks Giles, Tanya McGaha, Anne Butler, Cornelia Calhoun, Mary Clay, John Gray, Kim Lady Smith, Mary Winter, and Jim Wallace, who were among those serving on the steering committee. These initiators were joined by other willing hands that gathered photographs, coordinated copying, and provided oral history interviews. Among this group were the Clinton Street/Mayo-Underwood Reunion Committee and special long-time Black citizens. It was their enthusiasm, good will, concern, and, more than anything else, the sharing of memories, photos, and time that kept pumping new blood into the project as the time slipped by so quickly. Thanks for believing in us.

KHS staff Mary Winter and Kim Lady Smith never failed to respond to our on-going requests for more and more images and oral interview transcriptions and for databases and print-outs needed as the work progressed. Doug Boyd, KHS oral history archivist, conducted interviews and edited oral history excerpts for the book. J. Kevin Graffagnino, KHS executive director, and Melba Porter Hay, head of the Research and Publications division, took time from their busy schedules at KHS to edit later drafts. Only you could have provided us with the technical and editorial assistance needed, and for this I am most appreciative.

No work requiring lots of research can be possible without helpful, knowledgeable historians and librarians; in this case, our "in-house" historian, John Hardin, associate professor of history and assistant dean of Potter College of Arts, Humanities and Social Sciences at Western Kentucky University, took over the tedious task of compiling the "Chronology" when I became editor. The librarians were located at Kentucky State University, the Kentucky Department for Libraries and Archives, the Kentucky Historical Society Library, and for two years, at Miller Library in Ellicott City, Maryland. Archivist Betsy

Morelock at the Center of Excellence for the Study of Kentucky African Americans at Kentucky State University gave me access to several private collections and memorabilia that took me inside the lives of many Frankfort ancestors. She and Rhonda Watts, administrative assistant, were always gracious about my many interruptions. Of course, CESKAA director Anne Butler was my constant companion, on whom I depended for all kinds of help, from a willing ear to sound editorial advice. To all of you, I give thanks.

My deepest appreciation goes to those who volunteered to read, talk about, or listen to tapes of the early drafts of the narrative in order to clarify facts, spot omissions, provide missing pieces, and expand memories: Mother Mary Ellis, Margurite Shauntee, Henrietta Gill, Wallace Mitchell, Ora Mae Cheaney, Katie Jones, Catherine Graham, Sherman Collins, and others.

To Helen Exum, my neighbor, good friend, and extended family who kept the house during my two-year Maryland baby-sitting venture, who read and found something good to say about even the early bad drafts of the narrative, and who provided access to my kitchen table for my collaborators when they needed a quiet place for their "thinking points" to develop—to you, abundant love and gratitude. Without the thinking points that were later transmitted to me by telephone, e-mail, and anything moving east, and the loyalty and faith that only "laborers of love" can muster, this book could never have happened. Sheila Mason Burton and James E. Wallace performed editorial tasks willingly, joyfully, frequently at great sacrifice, while both continued to meet the demands of full-time employment.

To my loving family in Maryland, especially my daughter Betty, whose speed reading and sharp eye caught errors no one else would dare to point out; to my darling granddaughter, Olivia, who willingly took daily naps in order to give her Grammy thinking, reading, writing (sometimes napping) breaks and who gleefully traveled with me to the Miller Library to help find books and resources, my heart overflows with affection and adoration. When Olivia is able to read, I hope this book will be at the top of her reading list and that she will find in the joys of knowing her Frankfort past inspiration to keep the family going.

WINONA L. FLETCHER

Note: We who are distinguished by skin color in this country have had difficulty deciding what we prefer to be called or what to call ourselves. Arguments have been made for any one of a collection of labels over the years: Colored, People of Color, Negroes, Afro-Americans, Blacks, African Americans. Passionate appeals have also been made for capitalization of the preferred title in an attempt to avoid the stigma of inferiority attached to the "lower case" for proper nouns. In deference to the broad span of ages and diverse experiences of those who contributed to *Community Memories*, I, as senior editor, have chosen to use interchangeably several of the names we choose to call ourselves and to capitalize them all.

INTRODUCTION

The images and recollections featured in this book draw upon photographs and oral history interviews that were gathered through a truly community project. It started in the mind of John Gray of Historic Frankfort, Inc., in 1995. He developed a proposal to copy photographs from African American family collections, to preserve them, and to make them publicly accessible. He turned to the African American Heritage Commission, under the auspices of the Kentucky Heritage Council, who responded with enthusiasm. They provided initial funding for the project and were quickly joined in their support by the Franklin County Bicentennial Commission, the City of Frankfort, and the Farmers Bank and Capital Trust Co.

Gray then approached the Kentucky Historical Society and the Kentucky Oral History Commission for technical support. Seizing the opportunity to build on earlier KHS efforts, including the model "Ohio River Portrait" project, the landmark *History of Blacks in Kentucky,* and Assistant KHS Director James Wallace's work to document the history of the "Bottom" in Frankfort, the Society joined the project as a full partner. Expressing a keen interest in augmenting the photographs with personal recollections, the Kentucky Oral History Commission joined the effort by funding an oral history component to the project.

Although the institutional, financial, and technical support was in place, the project could succeed only if members of the community responded with a willingness to share their images and to tell their stories. Clearly, an effort designed to tap hidden resources in a close-knit community could flourish only if that community embraced the project. Frankfort native Sheila Mason Burton responded to the challenge by assembling a group of dedicated community volunteers, who served as core members of a project steering committee. When Mason Burton put out the call for help, Anne Butler, Cornelia Calhoun, Mary E. Clay, Bernice Combs, Mattie Davis, Winona Fletcher, Brooks Giles, Henrietta Gill, Clara E. Hogan, Dorothy Jones, Tanya McGaha, Dorothy McGowan, John Sykes, and Barbara White responded with untiring enthusiasm. The volunteers informed each phase of the project—from image collection and interviewing, to image selection for an exhibit at the Old State Capitol, and finally development of this publication—bringing their own perspectives and experiences from the community.

In the first phase of the project, community residents were invited to bring their photos to four copy sessions hosted at First Baptist Church, Corinthian Baptist Church, Kentucky State University, and the annual Clinton Street/Mayo-Underwood High School reunion. The Revs. K. L. Moore, L. A. Newby, and Edgar Mayham of the First Baptist, Corinthian Baptist, and St. John A.M.E. Churches encouraged their congregations to participate, while Cable 10 and Al Dix and Phil Case at the *Frankfort State Journal* spread news of the project community-wide. At each site volunteers recorded identifying information and Historic Frankfort volunteer Gene Burch, who loaned use of his own photographic equipment, made archival film copies. Burch and KHS photographer Nathan Prichard made over four hundred fifty copy images found in fifty-two personal collections, enhancing access to and preservation of a vital component of Frankfort's past.

As the photographic copy sessions came to a close, the oral history interviews became the project's focus. Oral history conveys life stories drawn from memory, prompted by an inquisitive interviewer, and recorded for posterity. The communication of life stories, remembrances, and experiences transforms a single memory into a shared entity. From the repetition and reconstruction of this shared memory emerges a sense of collective meaning, interpretation, and thus group identity. It is this identity that shapes, defines, and redefines the worldviews of the participants involved in the community created out of this social bond. When experiences and perceptions move from the mind of one individual to the shared memories of the collective group, the result is the formation of community memories.

These memories offer a brief glimpse into the everyday life of several Black individuals and communities in Frankfort, Kentucky. To say that there could possibly exist a singularly unified "African American community" in Frankfort is a challenging proposition. Within the city there have been multiple Black neighborhoods, within which are individual streets that develop vastly different personalities as residents come and go. There have been several Black churches, each with unique perspectives, and individual nuances in worship and musical styles. Prior to integration there were three Black schools, employing educators with different teaching styles, instructing students with diverse curricular and extracurricular interests. In addition, there were multiple families led by adults who worked hard in very different occupational communities, who, along with their children, lived in these neighborhoods and attended these churches and schools. Had we conducted one thousand interviews for the project, we would not have covered all of the potential perspectives.

We conducted interviews with thirty-seven individuals for the project. Initially, members of the steering committee identified, through personal networks of friends, family, and acquaintances, several individuals they felt should be interviewed. These individuals were contacted and interviews were scheduled. Unfortunately, as is the ever-present danger with oral history, some individuals passed away before they could be interviewed for the project. In rare cases, a few contacts declined an interview. However, in most cases, people were excited by the project and eager to participate. Winona Fletcher, Sheila Mason Burton, Jim Wallace, and Doug Boyd conducted the oral history interviews. From these interviews emerged several large themes expressing individuals' experiences about a shared past. Every person has a story and every story is different. Individuals perceive the same events and experiences through unique lenses of interpretation. In addition, individual memories fade as time passes and sometimes memories conflict.

Nowhere is this more evident than in the story of Ann Reed, a Black centenarian who was interviewed for a special newspaper edition during Frankfort's centennial in 1886. In that article, Reed, who claimed to be between 108 and 114 years old (born ca. 1771–78), told of her life during slavery, when she was "large enough to wait on the table" for General Washington, and how she remembered well the War of 1812. Her recollections of local interest included Frankfort (established in 1786) before any houses were built, General Lafayette's visit to Kentucky in 1825, and the 1826 hanging of Jereboam Beauchamp for the murder of Solomon P. Sharp. At the end of the interview, however, the newspaper made the disclaimer that Mrs. Reed's mind was fading and that she could be recounting tales of events she had heard described, rather than ones she had personally witnessed. Indeed, the 1880 Franklin County census cited her age as 99, which would have placed her birth closer to 1780–81. In any case, whether her accounts were eyewitness or hearsay, they unquestionably recalled an earlier time through a unique perspective.

The interviews and photographs gathered through this project reveal many deeply rooted traditions and group identities among Black residents in the Frankfort area. Celebrations, stories, songs, meeting places, rites of passage, and occupational lore create the fabric of community memory, reflecting common bonds, shared values, and visions.

The elusive concept of community is what binds together the chapters of this book. The chapters are mere conceptual lines, drawn from the dominant themes that emerged in the images and interviews. As we began to look more closely at the collection, we were struck by the sense of achievement, community, and belonging that emerged. The important roles of the churches, of the schools, of hard work, and of family were evident throughout. Intertwined within these recollected webs of social interaction are the memories of the neighborhoods, the businesses, and many individual personalities. However, a community consists of much more than geographical proximity or neighborhood closeness. The concept of community materializes from shared experiences, traditional knowledge and customs in common, communal rites of passage, religious expression and fellowship, the development of occupational folk groups, as well as the constant development and maintenance of the social bonds of family and friendship. What emerges is a common cultural frame of reference solely based on these social relationships.

Community Memories brings together a small collection of a shared past. Additional images pertinent to the Black experience in Frankfort are accessible in other KHS photo collections and other public repositories. Yet the compilers of this book made a conscious decision to constrain the scope of the book to the images and interviews collected through the project. As such, readers will find significant parts of Frankfort's Black history missing in this work. Personalities, events, and buildings that emerged repeatedly in the oral traditions were inexplicably missing from the photographs brought to the copy sessions. For example, although members of St. John A.M.E. congregation were heavily involved in the development of the project, very few images relating to the church came to the collection. Many of the photos that are included may seem technically lacking, yet they provide a candid insider's perspective.

Together, these images and shared remembrances reflect a strong sense of identity among Frankfort's Black residents and serve as a tribute to that group's shared experiences. This book commemorates the ongoing story of African American communities in Frankfort, Kentucky. Our hope is not to create a static memorial to the past, but to begin a dynamic dialogue about the past with the present. Those who wish to browse the entire collection will find the photographs and full transcripts of the interviews in the special collections research room at the Kentucky Historical Society. We encourage anyone who has photographs or recollections they would like to add to the project to contact KHS special collections.

Finally, the publisher would like to thank the senior editor, Dr. Winona Fletcher, for her untiring efforts to make this book a reality. Throughout the Community Memories Project, she gave countless hours and brought a dedication and focus that were crucial to the completion of this work.

THE PUBLISHER

Dr. Winona L. Fletcher at work on the Community Memories Project.

COMMUNITY MEMORIES

Mary L. McGee

Mason Burton: *Is there anything you miss about those good old days when you think about the Black community now, and the Black community then?*

McGee: *The togetherness…then, everybody was door, by door, by door, by door. Okay, when they started taking these houses [during urban renewal], today, I don't know where some of the people that lived next door to me live now. And, you don't have that togetherness because you scattered. You know, and people were there for you if you needed somebody.*

Camellia "Susie" Million and her sisters, Marcella and Patricia "Kitty," on Blanton Street in the mid-1950s.

Contributed by Barbara F. White

"BLEST BE THE TIES THAT BIND"

• COMMUNITY •

---

*"We lived together, fought with one another,
cried together, and other things
that make people close."*

James "Papa Jazz" Berry
Frankfort State Journal,
March 2, 1975

FRANKFORT'S AFRICAN AMERICAN community has been composed of many neighborhoods, each of which evolved at different times and for different reasons. Neighborhoods, like the people who live in them, tend to develop character—distinguishing features by which they become known. The settlements that have made up the Black community in Frankfort have all had their own unique traits. Among the earlier neighborhoods, Green Hill and Hickman Hill, located in the eastern portion of the county, were small and rural in nature, as was Farmdale in the southwestern part of Franklin County. Normal Heights, located in the area surrounding the Kentucky State Normal School (now Kentucky State University and subsequently referred to as Kentucky State), and often referred to simply as "The Hill," had an abundance of families and several small restaurants. "The Bottom," or "Craw," in downtown Frankfort was frequently flooded and housed many of the Black community's business, social, and religious institutions. The South Frankfort Black neighborhood at one time extended to the area surrounding the State Capitol but later became concentrated nearer the Kentucky River. Among the newer neighborhoods, College Park was started by a group of stockholders composed primarily of faculty and staff at Kentucky State. The only subdivision in Frankfort financed and built completely by Blacks, it encompassed a 32-acre tract that had once been part of the college's farm. Sutterlin Terrace on Douglas Street, and the Cherokee subdivision, across from Kentucky State, came about because of urban renewal.

Within the various Black neighborhoods, proximity, unity, and shared purpose presented numerous opportunities to socialize. A warm evening in any of these areas would find neighbors gathered on front porches sharing news and gossip, men congregating on street corners "shooting the breeze," and children playing in the street, most winding down after a long day and dinner around the kitchen table. Sounds of "Mother, May I?" and "Red Light/Green Light" emanated from the street and empty fields in South and North Frankfort, on the "Hill," and wherever children congregated to play. Images of girls jumping rope and playing hopscotch and boys shooting marbles and riding scooters caught the eye. At dusk, a mother's call from a porch or window signaled the end of the game—even if a new one had just begun. A sense of safety and security prevailed, where door keys were shared, if doors were locked at all. Margaret Berry explained, "We never had to lock a door…in the summertime…we'd leave the windows open…. We could go to sleep and we didn't have to worry about nobody because there was always somebody walking and watching."

Collective responsibility was an accepted way of life in the Black neighborhoods and that responsibility was extended to children and elders alike. In these multigenerational neighborhoods, the philosophy that "it takes a village to raise a child" found expression in the way adults monitored and disciplined youngsters, regardless of whether the children were theirs. James Ellis remembered "Old Miss Johnson" watching from her front porch over children playing ball along Hill Street. "Believe me, she'd referee. And she'd say…'You're out! You're out!' You'd just as well forget it!" Margaret Ellis added, "If we got out of line any way, somebody from somebody's porch would holler at us."

Not surprisingly, some elders in the neighborhood, though deeply loving and appreciative of the children, tended to be a little less tolerant of the noise and confusion that a street full of kids can create. On Third Street it was Ada Hudson; on Second Street it was Florence Warren. But, in general, as William Calhoun summed it up: "Everybody was everybody's child." Respect for older residents was common throughout the community of neighborhoods. In a world that was often challenging, if not oppressive, residents recognized and honored the strength and cunning that their elders employed to survive.

Despite their separate locales and distinct features, the neighborhoods inhabited by Blacks in Franklin County formed the total Black community. Issues significant to Blacks further united this community in action. Frankfort, as the state's capital, has often been a center for issues affecting African Americans throughout the state. Thus, local Blacks, by virtue of living at the center of state government, were often called upon to take leadership roles in organizing marches, protests, and community response. Forced together because of racism, or felt injustices, or when united for a common cause, Blacks in different neighborhoods were welded into the larger community by circumstances affecting all their lives.

Two causes that united the Black community were the threat to destroy Green Hill Cemetery and the civil rights movement of the 1960s, especially the early sit-ins and the 1964 March on Frankfort. Community leaders emerged from these events—people such as Jackson Robb, the Rev. Edgar Mack, Helen Holmes, Frank and Margurite Shauntee, Doctors Gus and Gertrude Ridgel, William Exum, Archie Surratt, John Buckner, the Rev. K. L. Moore, and Jimmy Graham, to name a few. Many were connected with Kentucky State, which has always served as a magnet to attract and develop strong leadership.

Margurite Shauntee, whose voice was frequently heard at tense moments during the days of the civil rights movement in Frankfort, remembered a time when she and Helen Holmes were driving home after a meeting and discovered a carload of disgruntled whites following their car. "Mrs. Holmes just cleverly headed for the Bottom, where she knew those white boys did not want to go; we came on home safely after that."

Religious, educational, business, and social institutions served as engines of the community. Community life and institutional life intertwined; the threads ran together to strengthen and reinforce each other. Local businesses—beauty and barbershops, grocery stores, nightclubs, and restaurants—served as meeting places where folks from the various neighborhoods shared news and talked with each other. The local churches, three of which were located in the Bottom, drew hundreds of Blacks together for Sunday and other weekly activities. Winnie A. Scott, the hospital that served the Black community, was located in South Frankfort and was the birthplace for many throughout the various neighborhoods. And, of course, the schools located in the Bottom and on the Hill—Clinton Street, Mayo-Underwood, Rosenwald, and Kentucky State— were perhaps the most treasured of all the community's institutions. Support for these institutions galvanized the entire community. Crowds turned out for dances, fashion shows, bazaars, community entrepreneur and entertainer Jack Robb's organ/piano concerts, and other fund-raising annual affairs. Some were noteworthy because of their novelty, such as the "Tom-Thumb Wedding" and "The Womanless Wedding," which saw Jack Robb, Will Wren, and a number of the community's men and boys in drag back in 1943. These were fun, community-oriented activities that not only raised money, but also helped weave together community life and institutional life.

Certainly the local clubs and organizations whose members came from throughout the Black neighborhoods were at the heart of community life. The Black community possessed a rich and varied set of social organizations that served as social outlets for both women and men. They were especially vibrant during the late nineteenth and early twentieth centuries when social outlets were sometimes restricted. Many were Frankfort specific—the Grad Club, Capital City Club, Jolly Eights, and Pleasurettes, and later the Jazz Moms, Ebonettes, Brickhouse, Brickettes, and New Direction. Others were local chapters of national organizations: American War Mothers, Women's Progressive Club, Links, Masonic Lodges, and fraternities and sororities. Frankfort-specific clubs have diminished in number, while local chapters of national organizations continue to exist and flourish.

Special individuals, sometimes lovingly referred to as "characters," also defined the community. Former residents of the Bottom remember "Squeezer" Brown with fondness. Brown, a World War I veteran and musician, could be seen playing and performing around the neighborhood and was famous for using his pension check to buy local kids treats that they could not otherwise afford. Residents of many of the Black neighborhoods were accustomed to friendly visits from "January," a gentle white man, and Eva Cox, both of whom sold "baseball tickets," a popular form of gambling. Most of the neighborhoods had their own beloved characters. Their antics and lifestyles lent personality to community life and created shared memories.

Communities evolve; they are not static. Sometimes they even die. The loss of a community can inflict tremendous emotional and spiritual scars. Such was the destruction of the North Frankfort "Bottom" neighborhood by urban renewal in the late 1950s and 1960s. Former residents expressed a sense of helplessness and loss of control of their lives, a feeling of unfairness and lack of concern for family and community. Margaret Berry summed it up this way: "They mistreated the people...took the school away [Mayo-Underwood].... If they'd let us alone, left our teachers alone, the school would have been there and our children would have learned something. Now they go to school....Those people don't care nothing about them. They don't push them. We got some [smart children] come out of Mayo-Underwood as lawyers and doctors and everything." Healing such wounds takes many years.

Today, as housing and residency patterns change, the traditional Black urban neighborhood is becoming a rarity. Well-defined Black neighborhoods are dwindling and the number of residents in them continues to diminish as individuals move out into surrounding suburbs. The neighborhoods adapted to changing needs and demands. In earlier years the barbershop, beauty parlors, bars, and clubs resonated with laughter and gossip. The street corners and front porches—the open windows and neighborhood fences—were once favorite meeting places. More recently, kitchen tables, churches, and club meetings, the Senior Citizen Center, and the YMCA provide places for shared memories, news, and gossip. While some of the old ways of connecting have been replaced, many are still alive and well in Frankfort's Black community. The old African commitment of "obligations to our people" remains a major motivation for action and also serves as the infrastructure of community dynamics among African Americans in the city.

William Calhoun

Frankfort...may have been quaint, but it was a very involved little town. Everybody knew everybody. Everybody was family.

Picnic for the community in the South Frankfort Park, sponsored by Mason's Grocery, 1986. Mary Chambers, Zuelia Waiters, Kenya Paris, John Medlock, Mary E. Ellis, George White Jr., Danny Clay.

Contributed by Andrew Mason Sr.

William Calhoun

We had a sense of community. We had a sense of pride. Kids' parents demanded and expected excellence.

James Calhoun

But you was still happy. You ate. You sacrificed. You gave your neighbor something if you had a garden; handed something over the fence. They'd bring you something. That made the outlook on life a little brighter.

George Wolfe, Claudia Roberts, Eddie Smith, and Robert H. Hogan; back: Madge Williams and Donna Fields, ca. 1962.

Contributed by Cornelia F. Calhoun

7

Children of Sutterlin Terrace (Douglas Street) and Green Hill who are members of the Sutterlin Terrace Junior Sanitarians Club, 1968. Unknown, Leslie Chisley, David Chisley, unknown, Ann Harshaw, unknown, Greg Harshaw, unknown, Calvin Samuels, unknown. Catherine Jones, sponsor, is in the background.

Contributed by Mary E. Clay

Margurite Shauntee

Fletcher: *Tell me a little about the early communities. You mentioned some early communities that I've heard no one else talk about. Where else did Black people live besides over there where you lived, over there on 2nd?*

Shauntee: *There was the "Craw" Section and then there was Green Hill and Hickman Hill. At one time you couldn't get to Green Hill only on the interurban unless you walked or had a car.... It went from Frankfort to Lexington; they called it the interurban and the Arcade Building right there at High before you get to the State National Bank, that's where the interurban used to come out, the office was there. And it had tracks that ran all the way to Lexington. You had to pay a dime to get to Green Hill.*

Clara E. Hogan

And we would walk back home up the hill—this was called Normal Heights at that time and we lived on "the Hill." We had three communities, South Frankfort, North Frankfort, and on "the Hill" was Normal Heights, and that's when Kentucky State first became "Normal School."

Mary Coleman, John Coleman, Loretta Longfoot Brown, and child Juanita Mae Brown standing in their yard in Hickman Hill neighborhood, 1928.

Contributed by Sheila Mason Burton

8

Clara E. Hogan

Hickman Hill was a Black community. And they had a little church—Methodist church out there, and when that settlement broke up they come to St. John, and some of our benches are from that little church and the clock is from Hickman Hill Church. So my mother and them, they all come to Frankfort and joined St. John Methodist Church.

William Washington

My grandparents lived in Green Hill—Mamie and George Graham. I would always go out there in the summer, and then when I was younger, I hated to go, because I thought that was the country and we lived in the city. We would go out there and visit for two weeks. Then I had a first cousin to come from Cincinnati, and we would always stay out there for at least two weeks—fishing or whatever.... We would ride what was called a city bus that would go to the top of old Mill—there was a mill up there in Green Hill—and then we would get out and walk.

Josephine Krank

Fletcher: *Can we continue talking a little about the communities and particularly South Frankfort and changes you've seen occur?*

Krank: *We're going back to the pattern of people moving wherever they want, because there were Blacks who lived on the lower end of Campbell St. and was a lady, Ms. Sue Paey, right behind where Noonan's was on the lower end of Shelby Street. And she kept almost anybody. It wasn't a transient thing, but people would come in who stayed a while. And, then, particularly on the upper end of Logan Street, adjacent to the Capitol, you know, Blacks used to live all up there. And they have just...recently torn those houses down, I think. But there was a community of Blacks up in that area.*

Robert Hogan and William Stone, sitting on the corner of Third and Murray Streets.

Contributed by Grace T. Harris

9

BLACK NEIGHBORHOODS

Historically, there were three predominantly Black neighborhoods in Frankfort, as well as several rural Black communities in Franklin County. The cohesive flavor of these neighborhoods has given way to the global trend toward less distinct boundaries and character.

North Frankfort – At different times, portions of North Frankfort were known as *Craw* or the *Bottom*, which was largely demolished by urban renewal in the 1960s. The neighborhood was bound by the river, Fort Hill, and the Old State Capitol.

South Frankfort – *Pawpaw Shoots*, owing its name to African tradition, was near the Capitol at Briar Cliff and Stanley Streets. Later, Black neighborhoods were concentrated north of 4th Street and east of Logan Street.

Kentucky State vicinity – *Normal Heights* was situated on "the Hill," adjacent to Kentucky State on the eastern side.

Douglas St. and *Sutterlin Terrace* (located in the Douglas St. circle) grew east of Kentucky State as the campus annexed land once a part of the Normal Heights neighborhood.

The *Cherokee subdivision*, and later, *College Park*, followed suburban development trends, growing south of Main St. and progressively farther from Kentucky State.

Rural Communities – *Green Hill* was essentially a rural community nestled southwest of US 60 where it curved to intersect US 460.

Hickman Hill was situated east of Frankfort, near the Woodford County line, along Leestown Road (US 421).

Farmdale was found south of Frankfort on the road to Lawrenceburg (US 127), near the Anderson County line.

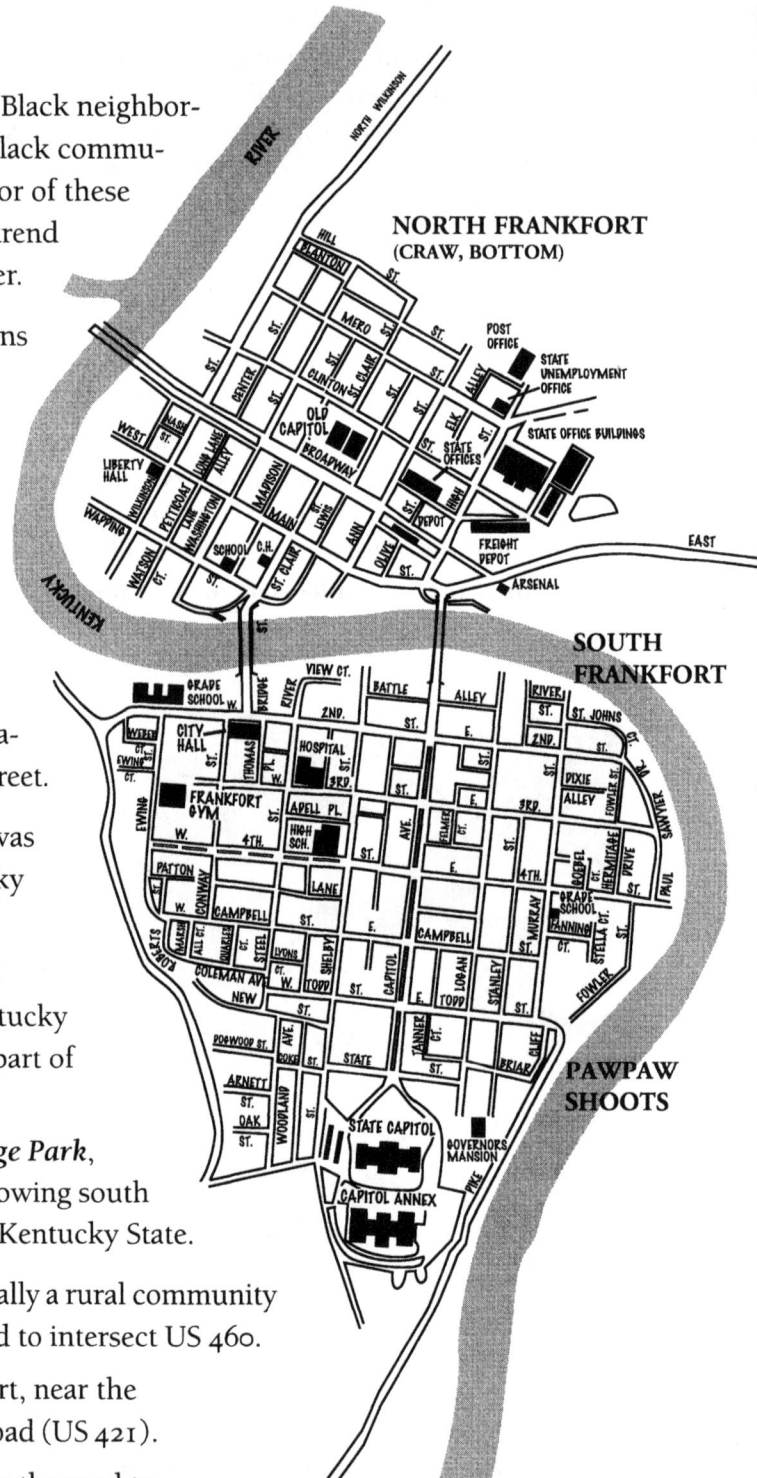

Map showing Black Neighborhoods in Frankfort and Franklin County

NORMAL HEIGHTS

SUTTERLIN TERRACE

THOMPSON ST
ROBINSON
DOWLAS ST
VALLEY VIEW PL.
DOWLAS AVE.

KENTUCKY STATE COLLEGE

COLLEGE SUWAY
COLLEGE ST.

SCHOOL

GOLD

K.S.C. ATHLETIC FIELD

HARBOR

MAIN

LANGFORD

MISSOURI AVE.

CHEROKEE AVE.

MAIN ST.

GREENHILL CEMETERY

ATWOOD

GREENHILL AVE.

VERSAILLES ROAD

GREEN HILL

AVE.

460

60

COLLEGE PARK

GOLD

ATWOOD PL.

HARBOR

PINES PL.

EXUM CT.

SEVEN

POTOMAC PL.

N W E S

Base derived from a 1959
Kentucky Department of
Highways map of Frankfort.

60

460

GREEN HILL

FRANKFORT

LEESTOWN PIKE

60

421

HICKMAN HILL

127

N W E S

Base derived from a 1929
Kentucky Geological Survey
map of Franklin County.

127

FARMDALE

Map showing Black Neighborhoods in Frankfort and Franklin County

Base derived from a 1959
Kentucky Department of
Highways map of Frankfort.

Base derived from a 1929
Kentucky Geological Survey
map of Franklin County.

The Odd Fellows Hall, later the American Legion, at the corner of Clinton and Washington Streets (looking east on Clinton and south on Washington). Ward Apartments also housed the People's Pharmacy in the 1910s.

Contributed by John Sykes

John Sykes

Boyd: *Let's start with some of your earliest memories of Frankfort.*

Sykes: *Well, I remember it wasn't very bright back then. They had little, small streetlights with just regular bulbs in them, almost. So after dark you had to run from light to light, you know, just to stay in visual, because it would get pretty dark. Real smoky, everybody then burned coal. I don't think there was any gas. Weren't any gas stoves in the neighborhood. And of course, you know there weren't any electric stoves back then.… A lot of people didn't even have refrigerators. They had what they called ice boxes. And the ice truck came around every day from the Frankfort Ice and Coal Company. The Sullivans…they would come by and you'd put a little sign up of what size piece of ice you wanted. And they would chop off a piece and they put it in, what they called the ice box and it would last for about a day. And we as kids would follow the truck and as they'd chip the ice off, we'd get the little pieces and suck on them. We'd follow the truck around through the neighborhood.*

Archie Surratt

Fletcher: *Were the areas/communities pretty much all Black and all white?*

Surratt: *The Craw area, a lot of people would make you believe that it was all Black—but it wasn't. There were a lot of white people there, and there was a relationship there that you've probably never seen anyplace else. Even the whites that were down there, they were part of it and they were "buddy-buddy." They were with you if you had troubles and so on.*

12

Margaret Ellis

*And at eight o'clock [p.m.], you was home…
we were all neighbors and friends. And
this time of year [summer], all of the old
folks would be on their porches.… If we
got out of line any way, somebody from
somebody's porch would holler at us.*

Mary Helen Berry

*We [were] like…one big family. Every-
body knew each other and we [were] just
close.… People would sit out on their
porch till it would cool off and they would
talk to each other.…It would be fun to
hear them,…and that's the way people
enjoyed themselves. [At] all the corners,
women would come from church or when
they'd get off work, they would meet on the corner and share the news. And it would be fun.*

Elizabeth Rodgers and Ella Greene relax
in front of a house on Murray Street.

Contributed by Barbara F. White

James Calhoun

*Getting back to the Bottom. It was a good place.… You could see everybody. You could go down and
sit on the corner. People come into town to see somebody, they would say, "Well, have you seen so-
and-so,"…[and] all you had to do was say, go down and sit on the corner of Clinton and Washington.
They'll be by. And they would…that day…everybody would come down. It was a friendly attitude.
Blacks and whites lived together. They would have their scrapes,…but they were in the neighborhood
and everybody looked out after each other.*

The City Federation of Frankfort,
Ky., shown here ca. 1940s, was formed
as a social and civic club. Standing at
rear: Mrs. Maurice Coleman, Etta
Blackburn; seated from left: unknown,
Mrs. Roberts, Laura Chase, Mrs. J. B.
Broaddus, Marie Robinson, Mrs.
Wyatt Thomas, Ada Carson, Katie
Hancock Brown, Mrs. George Hughes;
seated at right side: Julia Tracey,
Mrs. Manley, Mrs. J. Todd Simpson.
Others pictured are not identified.

Contributed by Mattie Davis

Mary Ellis

When you think about the past, down at the Bottom, we all lived down in the Bottom…just one big family.

Fannie Turner's dinner for friends at her home on Missouri Avenue in the 1960s. Hattie Lyons, Maggie Shannon, Nora Carter, Myrena Hall, Millie Combs, Fannie Turner.

Contributed by Clara E. Hogan

James Ellis

The water would come up all the time. And as kids, you know how kids are. We wanted the water to come, because we didn't have to go to school and, then we'd play around in the boats. We didn't have sense enough to know how that water was affecting families.… And that sewer down there, you know how the place got called the Craw…when the water would go down, there was a lot of crawfish right there.

James Graham

The…'37 flood, I rode in a boat with my father over the top of my house.

Mary L. McGee

I can remember that Big Flood. I always called it the Big Flood of 1937. And, the churches helped people to get out.

Washington Street, looking north, during the 1937 flood.

Contributed by Edna Rawlings Washington

14

The Madison Street junkyard, at the corner of Madison and Clinton Streets, looking west during the 1937 flood.

Contributed by Edna Rawlings Washington

Henry and Margaret Ellis

Henry Ellis: *I was living on Center Street during the '37 flood...a two-story house, and the water got up to the second floor and we came out the second story in a boat.*

Margaret Ellis: *Everybody would clean out their house and make a big fire and scrub the floors and things...and move right back in. Because you had nowhere else, you know. And then, down in there, a lot of people owned their homes. So, they wasn't just going to leave them.*

George Simmons

I found that, in the Bottom, when the water came up and everybody had to move out...it was just almost like having a convention or something.... They'd move out...have their drinks and everything. It was a celebration in a way. And...when the water went down, they'd go back in and start cleaning their houses out and having the same type of party.

The Oglesby backyard during the 1937 flood. Taken from the Old State Capitol yard.

Contributed by Edna Rawlings Washington

15

Second Street during the 1978 flood.

Contributed by Andrew Mason Sr.

The 1978 flood posed a greater threat to residents of South Frankfort than to those of North Frankfort.

Contributed by Andrew Mason Sr.

South Frankfort during the 1978 flood.

Contributed by Andrew Mason Sr.

Helen Holmes

We made our own social life.

A picnic on the Noel farm in the early 1950s. Clara Hogan in front, Mildred Chisley (against tree), and Emma White at right, with their children. The men at left are June White and George Chisley. Photographed by Bob Hogan.

Contributed by Clara E. Hogan

Clara E. Hogan

Fletcher: *You always lived on the "Hill." What did the families do for togetherness?*

Hogan: *Well, most of the time we had family picnics—every Sunday just about we'd all gather together and make homemade ice cream and bake pies, have ball games and just have a lot of fun…most of them were in the backyards; we didn't have too much transportation at that time, 'cause we didn't have a car; very few Blacks had cars—and we'd go out in the country.*

James Calhoun

We used to have shows in the backyard. Get people coming and just have fun and all. And mama was making some great big cake and we'd have ice cream. And all the neighborhood…sometimes there would be twenty or twenty-five people pitching horseshoes, kids playing.

Group on Murray and Third Streets, 1952. First row: Yvonne Thompson, Mary Jane Greenwood, Phenoleon Thompson Jr., Clarence "Baby Brother" Metcalf; back row: Phenoleon Thompson Sr. holding Toni Hogan, Eva Thompson, and Clara Hogan.

Contributed by Clara E. Hogan

Dr. and Mrs. B. T. (Helen) Holmes
at Links Club annual dance in the 1960s.

Contributed by Clara E. Hogan

Millie Combs

Mason Burton: *After you married and had your
kids, what did you do for entertainment?*

Combs: *We went to church socials, picnics, and
things outside and all, but we always done things
together, family things, and mostly
we would just go to one another's
house and sit around and talk and
play music and talk about everybody
and all my sisters, always, we all
went to my mother's on Sunday.*

Senior Citizens gathering at the
Kentucky State University Alumni House
during the mid-1960s. Sitting: Mrs. Jessie
Roach, Mary Williams, Corrine Beckley,
Marguerite Campbell; standing: Lucas Bush.

Contributed by Barbara F. White

Senior Citizens Party.
Seated: Martha Adams, Pearl Maxberry,
Odessa Hayes; standing: Callie Weathers,
Catherine Coleman, and Clintie Ellis.

Contributed by Cornelia F. Calhoun

Mary Helen Berry

Kozy Korner, that was up in the Bottom somewhere. Well, it was just a place where the young people and the older people sat and went to drink, or eat a good sandwich, or drink a cold beer. It was just a place where you met friends. It was a clean place.

George Simmons and
Henry Sanders

Sanders: *Down in the Bottom, to entertain...that's the only place you had to go. The joints, they had about six or eight different joints....*

Simmons: *You could go from one... to another. You could...walk out of one door and you [hear] the music...next door. They had a jukebox in every one of those.*

George Bowen, Al Boffman, and Robert Hayden in front of Mason's Grocery at the corner of Third and Murray.

Contributed by Andrew Mason Sr.

Sanders: *Kozy Korner was one. And, then, they had the 99 Club across the street. The Blacks and whites up and down the street...very seldom ever seen a fight between them or anything.*

Simmons: *And people would drive their cars along and they didn't have to get out of the cars, just roll their windows down and look at the people passing....They were enjoying everything.*

Restaurant upstairs over Mason's Grocery. This was a popular pool hall and party spot during the 1970s and 1980s. Jesse James, James Dematra, James "Wheat" Henderson, Ronnie Dean, Alonzo Graham; Mary Gladys Tillman holding pool stick.

Contributed by Andrew Mason Sr.

Group in front of The Grill restaurant on Washington Street, after Sunday morning church, 1948. Mary Virginia Burns, Joe Buddy Taylor, Juanita Clay, Elizabeth Boyd Graves, Henry Mack, Annie Mae Wren McClain, Anna Belle Berry Combs, A.C. Pollard (kneeling), James "Papa Jazz" Berry (holding dog). Photographed by James "Buddy" Ellis.

Contributed by Henry Mack

Barbara White

White: *Well, we can start with Tony Papa's and the library was right next door to Tony Papa's. He made ice cream. And he would come around on a truck and sell it. But we'd go up to his house and get it. And you know, you'd have to knock on the gate. Somebody would come and open the gate. And somebody would come out—a nickel a dip. We'd scrounge to get that nickel. We'd sell pop bottles. We'd collect rags and take them up to the junkyard. It wasn't really a lot of money, but you didn't do without. But Tony Papa's, oh, he did, nobody can top Tony Papa's ice cream.*

Boyd: *What was so good about it?*

White: *It was just good. Good and creamy. And the library was right next door to Tony Papa's. I was a reader and I'm still a reader. And when we didn't have anything else to do and when it was raining, we'd go to the library and they'd let us come in. We'd go sometimes after school to get our homework. In fact, I ended up working for the library for a while. I didn't get paid for it, but I worked up there. I covered for the lady that worked up there. But I think I read every Nancy Drew book and Hardy Boys book they had in the library.*

20

The Domestic Economy Social Club. Katie McClain, Mrs. Williams, Ann Brown, Sallie Fields, Atha Mitchell, Myrenia Hall, Serilda Guy, and Lucy Anderson.

Contributed by Josephine W. Krank

Josephine Krank

Fletcher: *Talk a little bit about…what Blacks did—do still—for entertainment and as social beings? Go back to some of the clubs.*

Krank: *You're talking about the Domestic Economy Club. Now that was a group of women. But they would get together and, I know they did civic work; their dues weren't much. I know they would sew sometimes, and they entertained each other. I think they just went from house to house. It was a means of their kind'a getting together with people their own age.*

Fletcher: *Did they choose the name "domestic" because most of them were?*

Krank: *I don't know—there is a possibility, but most of them were domestics—*

Fletcher: *When did it cease to be? Or is there a follow-up of it now?*

Krank: *No, I don't think there is a follow-up of it now; I don't know exactly when, but, most of the members were older when they joined, and I think they just sort of died.*

The Domestic Economy Social Club, February 1957. Maggie Jones, Cora Scott, Lucille Harris, Atha Mitchell, Serilda Guy, Amy Cherry, Loyella Clelland, Ann Brown, and Annie Stone.

Contributed by Josephine W. Krank

THE COLORED CHURCHES OF FRANKFORT

By Dr. E. E. Underwood, published in the *State Journal*, October 3, 1936.

The First Baptist Church was organized in 1833, its first pastor being Rev. Henderson Williams. Its members worshiped in a building on Clinton Street, adjoining the prison walls, and they continued to worship there until 1904. They then purchased its present site. Some opposition was encountered to the erection of the building in that neighborhood, some of the property holders going so far as to take the matter into the courts. The case was carried to the Court of Appeals, which handed down an unanimous decision sustaining their rights to build. Most of its ministers have enjoyed long pastorates, especially Rev. James Monroe, Rev. Robert Martin, Rev. Eugene Evans, and Rev. W. H. Ballew, its present pastor is the Rev. J. W. Broaddus who has been serving the church for over four years. This church owns its parsonage, located on Clinton Street, and an Annex building, fronting on High Street. This latter building is used for the various activities of the church, and contains a nice library. This church celebrated its 100th anniversary three years ago, which was a period of great rejoicing among its members.

The Corinthian Baptist Church, located on Mero Street, was organized in 1876. Its first pastor was the Rev. James H. Parrish. In 1929, under the pastorate of the Rev. W. L. Campbell, an Annex was built which contains a Sunday School room downstairs, and a pastor's study and seven additional rooms upstairs, which are used for the various activities of the church. Its present pastor is the Rev. L. V. Jenkins. It numbers among its pastors Rev. Reuben Strauss, Rev. R. H. C. Mitchell, Rev. William A. Credit, Rev. E. T. Fishback. This church owns its parsonage, which is located on Murray Street.

The St. John A.M.E. Church, located on Clinton Street, was organized in 1839, its first building being on Lewis Street. Its first pastor was the Rev. George Harlan. In 1893 the present building was erected under the pastorate of Rev. James M. Turner. About fourteen years ago an Annex was built, containing a Sunday School room, pastor's study and rooms for the activities of the church. Among its most prominent pastors were Rev. B. F. Lee, afterwards a Bishop in the Church, Rev. G. H. Schaffer, Rev. D. F. Bently [sic, Rev. D. S. Bentley], Rev. P. A. Nichols, Rev. G. F. David, Rev. J. W. Frazier. Its present pastor is the Rev. H. H. Brewer, who has been serving for a number of years. This church owns its parsonage which is located on Lewis Street.

Bethel Temple Apostolic Church is located on Washington Street, and is pastored by the Rev. Lula Jones. This church was organized in recent years. It is connected with the national organization of the same belief.

Fiftieth Anniversary Dinner of the Women's Progressive Club, Saturday, June 11, 1983. The dinner was held at the Winner's Circle, Capital Plaza Hotel. First row: Marianne Hanley, Jennie Mae Buckner, Lillie Blackburn, Julia Tracy, Anna Mary Wolfe, Anna Laura Ellis; second row: Henrietta Carpenter, Ora Mae Cheaney, Rose Henry, Helen Exum, Helen Holmes, Mildred Jacobs. Anna Belle Williams and Margurite Shauntee were absent when the photo was taken.

Contributed by Mattie Davis

Josephine Krank

Fletcher: *Progressive Women's Club was not a continuation of it?*

Krank: *No, because the Progressive Women's Club, now I think these women wanted to do civic work and those kinds of things, and it was a social club too. And there used to be another club around here —see I'm remembering all these things—"Maids and Matrons."*

Fletcher: *Oh, interesting. There were both married and unmarried—*

Krank: *Now that was strictly a social club because they would meet for card parties and have dances and those kinds of things. And I'm trying to think, it seems to be, I don't know whether the Chums Club is sort of a child of the Maids and Matrons or not—I believe it is. I'm not sure of that.*

American War Mothers convention, at First Baptist Church, Clinton Street. First row: 1 – Beulah Watson, 4 – Sallie Fields, 6 – Louise Simpson, 7 – Lucy Harth Smith, 8 – Odessa Hayes; second row: 5 – Beatrice Greene, 8 – Evelyn Williams; third row: 8 – Mrs. Andrew Coleman; back row: 2 – Maggie Warren, 3 – Cora Jones Redd.

Contributed by Cornelia F. Calhoun

Order of Eastern Star at Mayo-Underwood School. First row: left, Odessa Hayes; third from left, Alfred Million Jr.; fourth from right, Mrs. Carr Lee Calhoun; second row: third from left, Sallie Fields; third row: Betty Davis, unknown, Laura Bell Clay, Pearl Maxberry, Evelyn Williams, unknown, Mary Jones, Mrs. Sadie Caldwell, Cora Harris, Edna Washington; fourth row: Alice Williams King, Mabel Morton; fifth row: Louise Simpson, Laura Chase, unknown, unknown, Rev. William R. Hutchison, Gladys Hutchison, unknown, Anna Bell Williams, Rev. Andrew White.

Contributed by Barbara F. White

George Simmons and Henry Sanders

Simmons: *There was another club that men and women belonged to…*

Sanders: *Well, that's Town and Country Club, and, of course, Capital City Club; they're still in existence.…They had formed… about 40 years ago…and our purpose was to help anybody in the community that needed…help, like if somebody got burnt out or something. Or, a child needs clothing or somebody needs food.*

24

A Grad Club traditional gingham and jeans dance at the Stagg Distillery in the 1950s. Kneeling: Alfred Million, Henry Green, William Hume, Booker T. Holmes, Henry Mack, Henry Kemp, and Cecil Warren. Standing: Sylvester Krank, Ewing Atkins, Jesse Hale, Chester Brown, Edwin Moses, James Brown Sr., Robert "Plug" Williams, R. Carsons, Jack Robb, Ernest Payne, and George Simmons.

Contributed by Josephine W. Krank

Josephine Krank

Fletcher: *Was the Grad Club kind of comparable for the men to some of these that the women belonged to?*

Krank: *I believe the Grad Club was formed to help subsidize sports for the school, but then it evolved into more or less a social thing.*

Fletcher: *I was going to ask you when you said the women's clubs sponsored dances—where did they go to—back to the schools for those or were there club houses?*

Krank: *They have more or less always been able at some point to use Staggs.*

Grad Club party at the Stagg Distillery in the 1950s. Flora Bell Wade, Chester Brown, unknown, Ida Mae Calhoun, Alice Sanders King, Mary Alice Brown, Ethel Walker, and Dorothy Sanders (seated).

Contributed by Barbara F. White

Grad Club in 1969. Front row: George White Jr., Jay Spencer, Dr. William Exum, Chester Brown, James Patton, Andrew Mason, Clarence Williams, Jessie Hale; back row: George Simmons, Henry Sanders, John Sykes, James Brown, Frank McGowan, Henry Mack, Dr. B. T. Holmes, Leroy Dixon.

Contributed by Henrietta Gill

Josephine Krank

Fletcher: *What about the VFW? Was that Black-owned? What are some of the veteran's organizations?*

Krank: *The VFW, the American Legion…they used a building over on Clinton Street for a long time.… I remember the AKA's having something there at the American Legion one time.*

Chester Brown receives a plaque of appreciation and a life membership from the Grad Club. Mr. Brown was a charter member of the Grad Club. Standing: Van Warren, George White Jr., Dr. B. T. Holmes (with certificate), Paul Graham, James Patton, Charles Fields, Henry Sanders, Sterling Evans, Leroy Dixon; sitting and kneeling: Chester Brown (with plaque), Andrew Mason Sr., John Sykes, Clarence Williams.

Contributed by Andrew Mason Sr.

Sunday afternoon at the old American Legion, Clinton and Washington Streets. Ellsworth Marshall, Samuel Parker Jr., Ernest Wright, Richard Holton, Robert Sanders, Chester Brown, and Alex Sanders Sr.

Contributed by Ella Parker Sanders

Beta Upsilon Omega Chapter of Alpha Kappa Alpha Sorority, Inc., in the early 1950s.
Front: Josephine Krank, Margaret Baker, Pauline Gould, Odessa Green, Henrietta Morris.
Standing: Helen Exum, Dorothy Wilson, L. C. Spencer, Clara Smith, Mary Lynem, Mabel Atwood, Anna Surratt, Winona Fletcher, Charlotte Wilson, and Lillian Wright.

Contributed by Archie L. Surratt

Josephine Krank

Fletcher: *Well, now that you've mentioned the AKA, when did you join Alpha Kappa Alpha?*

Krank: *Oh, that was about 1934–35...that was the time when if you were a Greek in Frankfort, you were an AKA.*

Alpha Kappa Alpha (AKA) Sorority at the old Holiday Inn Founder's Day celebration, ca. 1983. Beta Upsilon Omega Chapter.

Contributed by Josephine W. Krank

Members of the Frankfort Alumnae Chapter Delta Sigma Theta Sorority, Inc., gathered on Memorial Day in 1992. Front: Gertrude Ridgel, Virginia Cofield, Brenis Taylor, Delores Graham, and Mary Fields; back: Kathy Peale, Hettie Oldham, Penelope McClain, Carrie Lasley, and Maria Lasley.

Contributed by Gloria Giles

Rose of Sharon group.
Contributed by Bessie B. Bright

The "Deltas" on retreat in 1997. Front: Gertrude Ridgel, Reneé Carter, Virginia Cofield, and Nichelle Davis; back: Mary Fields, Gloria Giles, Penelope McClain, and Vivian Lasley-Bibbs.

Contributed by Gloria Giles

29

James Calhoun

Yes, there's always been…a lot of prominent Black [social] clubs. My father, I'd see his uniform and swords…for the K of Ps [Knights of Pythias]. And that building down there [American Legion Building, corner of Washington and Clinton] was built by the old lodge people, the old American Legion building in the Bottom.… We'd go down and watch them parade and drill. The old men with their uniforms and their big swords.

PRIDE OF FRANKFORT. CO. No. 15. K. OF P.
FRANKFORT. KENTUCKY.

Knights of Pythias group, ca. 1905.
Contributed by Bill Feldman

Freemason group on the steps of the First Baptist Church. Front row: J. T. Harris, Frank Bush, and John Sykes; second row: Bill Jones, Louis Hall, Henry Davis, unknown, unknown, George White, and Jesse James; third row: Clarence Williams, James Clay, and James Jacobs Sr.; fourth row: Richard Hawkins, Donald Townsend, and Bill Stone.

Contributed by John Sykes

Capital City Lodge #1597, Industrial Legion Lodge #3102, Frankfort, Ky. Household of Ruth #170, Juvenile Society #540. Taken in front of Pythian Building (Oddfellows Hall), corner of Clinton and Washington Streets in 1917.

Contributed by Mary E. Ellis

The Bricketts, Thursday Night Women's League and Tournament winners, 1982. Front row: bat boy James Johnson, Hope Tillman, Barbara Reed, Sharon Chisley, Jeannie Carter, Sharon Yett, Joette Johnson, Linda Tillman; back row: coach John Sykes, Roberta Clay, Gloria Brown, Louise Jackson, Debbie Hogan, Gloria Washington, Carrie Watts, Teresa Graham, coach Ike Yett.

Contributed by John Sykes

John Sykes

Just some guys in the neighborhood that wanted something to do. They started playing on the field up at Kentucky State. And teams around town, I mean some guys down here, picked out a team, got a team together and they started playing against the guys on the campus and all around.... Really they weren't very organized, because I played on one team today and next time I'd go up there, whoever was short, I would play on theirs. So they decided they would get organized and get into the league....

They decided that they needed a coach. So, I decided to be the coach.... They used to let us in tournaments around here, just to see if we could get ten on the field. They knew that a big crowd would follow us, because when we left town and went to a game, there might be a hundred, a hundred and fifty people would follow us.... And then we'd start playing around Lawrenceburg, Danville, Harrodsburg. Everybody seemed to have a Black team. And that was a Sunday outing.... They'd pack their coolers and

32

The Mighty Brickhouse, a community social club that supported a softball team and contributed to many community and charitable activities. This team won the Tuesday night recreation Men's League championship in 1982. Back row: Ike Yett, Jerry Wade, Ricky Yett, Eugene White, L. J. Brown, George Gipson, Richard Hawkins; front row: assistant coach Elmore "Rooster" Alderson, Burnett Brown, Mike "Stroker" Johnson, Robert "Bobby" Redding, Charles Bowen, head coach John Sykes.

Contributed by John Sykes

their lunches and they'd follow us around wherever we went. And then the guys said this is the Brickhouse.

They said, well, if you've got a Brickhouse, the girls wanted to play. So, they started the Brickettes, because a lot of them had girls' teams. So we'd take the girls along. Now the girls were better than the guys. Our girls went on to the state [championship tournament]. Our guys never could even get out of the district. We'd win our little league, our class league.... We had a good time. We did a lot of traveling, met a lot of people. Gave people something to do.

The Brickhouse wasn't just a softball team. It was an organization. We even made donations to other civic organizations. On Christmas and Thanksgiving, we'd fix dinners and take around to unfortunates. We worked at some of these old houses around here.... We're still going. We still do the Christmas thing. But all of us got old.... They had so much pride in Brickhouse.

33

Henry Sanders

The first time I ever knowed "Squeezer" Brown we was living on Clinton Street, and I was going to the Clinton Street High School; [I was] in kindergarten. And "Squeezer" was painting an old house on the corner there. And that sun got hot. He came down off the ladder and looked up at the sun, went home and got his guitar and came back and got to picking on the guitar and said, "I don't bother work and work don't bother me." Of course, I was very young and it amazed me. He got his pension from the First World War and…he'd get a bunch of kids and he'd march with them you know. Like they was in the army. They had to march. And he'd march them to Tigers Inn and that's where the kids hung out…. And he'd have the man lock the door and then get anything they wanted in Tigers Inn. Now, if they didn't act right, they couldn't get nothing. But if they acted right, they'd get pop and ice cream and candy, anything they wanted. And they said he spent most of his pension on those kids.

John Robert Davis Jr., in zoot suit, 1941. Davis later operated a barbershop and restaurant on Washington Street in the old American Legion Building.

Contributed by Mattie Davis

James "Squeezer" Brown playing guitar.

Contributed by Nell Cox

James Calhoun

Wallace: *Do you remember Eva Cox?*

Calhoun: *Oh, my gosh, yes, indeed. Had a dog, and sold baseball tickets [essentially a lottery ticket for betting on baseball games]…Miss Eva Cox. "Squeezer" made up a song about her. And she got mad and was going to take him to court and sue him, and he was singing about Eva and oh, what a song.*

Wallace: *Do you remember how it went? Any of the song?*

Calhoun: *No, I can't remember it. Me and brother, the brother that died last, he and I said we was going to sit down and put the words in like we think it is, what he said about old Eva and oh, man, it was something. It was something.*

Barbara White

Boyd: *Miss Eva Cox, did you remember her?*

White: *Miss Eva Cox lived across the street from my grandmother.… But my grandmother never refused to let Miss Eva come in her kitchen and give her some breakfast or a cup of coffee.… But Miss Eva, she could be kind, but most of the time people picked at her. And she had dogs. She had, I bet you, ten or twelve dogs in her house. And I can remember she had one big dog that stood about this tall. It was a three-legged dog. But she sold those baseball tickets. Miss Eva sold baseball tickets. It was a book and then you'd just pull them. As a kid they didn't mean anything to us. But I mean, she'd have a pocket-book about like that, that would just be stuffed. And I guess, I guess when you'd win something she'd pay you off. But people would buy them, they'd buy them from her.*

Boyd: *Where did she live? Do you remember?*

White: *She lived on Wilkinson Street. Let me see. She lived next door to the Ellises, Buddy Ellis. And her house set kind of back in her yard. She had a big yard. Because I can remember a big oak tree in the front yard. And Buddy Ellis and them would make sure that Miss Eva had food.*

James Calhoun

Jack Robb was on the corner right there where the Civic Center is. They were the …well, only Black [funeral home]. Very, very prominent. Very…very well to do.

Margaret Ellis

And Jack had a dancing school. Upstairs in his mama's place, because I used to belong to it. He was a good entertainer, a good piano player, too. He didn't charge us…but a quarter.

Jackson Robb playing the organ. He owned the Robb Funeral Home, located on Clinton Street.

Contributed by Josephine W. Krank

35

Womanless wedding, a fund-raising production put on at Mayo-Underwood School by Jack Robb, 1943.
All of the persons in the picture dressed as females are Frankfort men and boys. Little boy who is dressed as a
boy with striped T-shirt is Mason Harris (first row). Also included in first row: Moses Sims (at far left end),
Isaac "June" Greene and Charles "Son" Wade ("flower girls" in center), Richard Williams (at far right);
second row: Rev. Utterback (holding baby); third row: Will Wren (bride in center), Sterling Evans (next to
Wren on right), Thomas Penny (next to Evans); top row: Jack Robb (in strapless dress), Jimmy Fields
(to bride's left), Squeezer Brown (three persons to bride's right).

Contributed by Mary E. Ellis

Helen Holmes

*Jack and I were really close. When we were getting ready for that
[Martin Luther King Jr. visit to Frankfort] we mapped out certain
homes…rest homes for people who were waiting. Jack was very
involved. He was a very fine pianist.… He was trusted by his Black
friends. He never sold out to anybody. Jack was a dependable person.*

Tom Thumb Wedding that was a fund-raising program for Mayo-Underwood
School, ca. 1938. Dorothy Gaines and Alex Sanders Jr. on Clinton Street.

Contributed by Alex Sanders

Dr. Edward E. Underwood, ca. 1915.

Contributed by Mary J. Robinson

Henry Sanders

Underwood was a doctor, Black doctor in Frankfort. And he was very well liked and born a lot of Black children around Frankfort. And he made house calls.

Margaret McIntosh

Boyd: *What year were you born?*

McIntosh: *Nineteen thirty-three. May the 18th, 1933, here in Frankfort, Kentucky. I was born at home, because back then, there was no hospital for the Blacks to go to, unless it was an emergency. And if it was an emergency, they had to go in the back way and be operated on and after they recovered, they'd bring them back out and take them home.*

Winnie A. Scott, at right, in front of the Winnie A. Scott Hospital.
A historic marker stands at the site of the hospital.

Contributed by Josephine Calhoun

37

Neighborhood kids standing at end of Second Street looking onto Paul Sawyier Drive, 1952. Cecil Drake in stroller; front row: Elisse Brown, Donna Marshall, Delores Brown; second row: Andrew Mason Jr., Sheila Mason, Bobby Mason, Camille Drake, Esten Collins, Cerdan Collins.

Contributed by Sheila Mason Burton

William Calhoun

When I went to Mayo-Underwood School I really began to understand what segregation was. We could get on the city buses. We didn't have to go to the back of the bus. I don't remember that in Frankfort. But I do remember Miss Addy telling me one day, "You know, you're supposed to come back here and sit." I said, "Well, I ain't"...you know, when I was a kid,..we've been able to sit up where we want to. But because she was a grownup I did what they asked. But we never had to go to the back of the bus.

Helen Holmes

When they started with [integrating] the swimming pool...I was head of the NAACP and we used to have quite an active group. We sat-in many a time. Only one person ever got arrested.... That was down at the drug store on the corner. Main Street. Well, that's...where a young man was arrested. We had a lawyer from Versailles, Ed Prichard. He was my advising lawyer. I said, "I don't mind having to get them out from being arrested, but I don't want them to do foolish things."

Group of South Frankfort kids playing in the parking lot on the Capitol grounds, ca. 1957. Don Marshall Jr., Donna Marshall, Sheila Mason, Toni Brooks, Elisse Brown, Delores Brown.

Contributed by Katie Johnson Graham

Virginia "Ducky" Brooks and Marjorie Doneghy playing dress-up in a yard on Third Street, 1957.
Contributed by Marjorie Doneghy Willis

William Calhoun

Calhoun: *When March the 5th [1964]…came,…do you remember that?*

Mason Burton: *Yes,…that's the day that Martin Luther King came.*

Calhoun: *Yes, and you remember we had that big march on Capital Avenue…. Black folks came from everywhere. I ain't never seen so many Black folks. 'Course I always saw a lot because I was with the college. You know, Rosenwald was above the college…. The people at the college was a culture up there that was all its own.*

Campus children at play near faculty apartments, June 1964.
Carol Surratt, Eddie Smith, Janet Smith.

Contributed by Archie L. Surratt

39

Halloween party given by Mason's Grocery for community kids, 1981.
The party was held in the upstairs portion of the grocery store.

Contributed by Andrew Mason Sr.

Mary Lucy McGee

Mason Burton: *What types of things did you and your brother and your sister and the other kids in the neighborhood do for entertainment?*

McGee: *Well, the main thing the girls did was jacks. We loved to play jacks. We'd sit on that porch and play jacks all day long, and brother and them would be on scooters out of milk carton boxes. Then milk come in the wood cartons, and they would take the skate wheels off the old skates and build these scooters, and they would let us ride them every now and then. And, of course the boys' game was marbles at that time. They would sit and play marbles all day long.*

Mary Helen Berry

We played in the streets. We played ball. We played marbles. Girls played marbles as well as boys.... Because a lot of my people lived on Wilkinson Street, I played with more white children than I did with Colored children because we all played together.

William Calhoun

So, I vividly remember how we could not go to the school at Murray Street, but we always played on the playground. That was a great hub of activity. The grown folks would be on the corner of Murray and Third. The children would be up at the playground. Across from Dr. Holmes's house was a field that was there, next to the Marshalls, and there used to be a little hill there, and we used to call it Little Mountain. We used to play baseball and softball in that field. Uh, even sometimes the white children would come and play. And they would basically have to sneak and do it. Or it was done in such a, almost a surreptitious way, you know. So we had a great life. Kids were creative.

Glenn Douglas

We'd go to the movies and whatever movie we saw that day, we'd go home and play.... If we saw a cowboy movie, we played cowboys. If we saw an Indian movie, we'd make bow and arrows, and if we saw a swashbuckler movie with knives and swords, we'd sword fight....

Franklin County playground closing festivities, 1972. Billy Davis, winner of the Soap Box Derby, and Queen Lylia McGowan are congratulated by Steve Brooks, city recreation director.

Contributed by Dorothy C. McGowan

We acted out everything we saw just about. And we had a good time doing these things, you know.... We'd go to the movies just about every time the theatre would change. It would only cost us fifteen cents, and I went until I was about twelve before Ms. [Roberta] Wilson, who was a theatre attendant there, caught up with the idea that I had gotten older, and I had to pay forty cents to go to the movies. We'd go to the movies and we'd sit in the balcony. The Caucasians or the white folks would sit downstairs. And we used to get put out of the movies a lot. We'd sneak in. We'd get bad. We'd watch the movie. We'd throw things downstairs. We'd throw popcorn, water, or whatever we felt like doing, you know. And Ms. Wilson would come and put us out. We'd already seen the movie anyway.... We had a good time. And we were always at the theatre. On weekends we'd go and take our girlfriends. Saturday, me and Kermit [Williams], we'd go to the movies a lot. And we'd meet girls there.

Clara E. Hogan

Fletcher: *Talk about...social life and what was going on in the city. What was there available to young Blacks—or to older Blacks?*

Hogan: *Not too much for younger Blacks. At one time they did have a skating rink that younger Blacks [were admitted to], but they weren't admitted to the "Y" at that particular time. And the movie theatres, the Capital and the Grand, and of course the Blacks were seated in the balcony. You would go up off of the street—now this was the Grand Theatre... upstairs and Mrs. Wilson...she took up the tickets and she stood in the hallway; it was very nice and you'd go on around and there you are at the balcony. Okay. Now the whites went off another area and straight on into the theatre.*

Fletcher: *Do you remember any of the movies?*

Hogan: Gone With the Wind; *we stayed all day long, took lunches in brown paper bags.*

Brownie Scout troop at day camp.
Contributed by Kevin Mason

AFRICAN AMERICAN SCHOOLS IN FRANKFORT, KENTUCKY

Frankfort area Blacks counted access to exemplary schools among the blessings of living in the capital city community. Among the most important institutions:

Clinton Street School for Colored Students – Following the Civil War efforts to educate local youth gained momentum with the funding and construction of this school in the mid-1880s. Located on East Clinton Street behind Kentucky State penitentiary, the school's principal, Professor William H. Mayo, led the institution, which served area children through 1928.

Mayo-Underwood School – Opened in 1929, this combined elementary and high school replaced Clinton Street and was named in honor of Professor William Mayo and Dr. Edward E. Underwood. It stood at the corner of Mero and Center Streets in the North Frankfort neighborhood and was the center of community life. It operated until 1964 and the advent of integration.

Rosenwald School, located since 1954 across East Main St. from Kentucky State University, began in 1908 as a model laboratory school for teacher training for the students of Kentucky Normal and Industrial Institute. It functioned as an elementary school for African American

Wesley "Joe" Marshall

Mason Burton: *Well, what do you miss about the good ole days?*

Marshall: *Oh, running up and down the street.... We'd go to the picture show and that's what I miss, going to the picture show. You could walk up there in town to the picture show, you know.*

Mason Burton: *You could go to the Grand, you couldn't go to the Capital. Did that ever make you mad?*

Marshall: *No, it never did bother me. Because we couldn't go the Capital, but we could go to the Grand and the Grand Alley, and later on, well, it got to where we could go to the Capital. But it didn't bother us.*

Brownie Scout Betty Fletcher with Kentucky State College President Rufus Atwood, ca. 1958.

Contributed by Winona L. Fletcher

---

students in the community as well as for children of KNII faculty and staff. In 1917, with support from the Rosenwald Fund, established by Sears, Roebuck, & Co. president Julius Rosenwald, a new building was constructed for $6,000, and the name was changed to Rosenwald. After this structure burned, the Rosenwald Fund helped build a new structure that served the school from 1923 until 1954, when the present building was erected. After integration, the school became a preschool institution, the Rosenwald Center for Early Childhood Development.

Kentucky State University has been a part of the capital city since its creation in 1886. Originally the State Normal School for Colored Persons, Kentucky State University is a unique liberal-studies, land-grant institution. The school is located on a bluff overlooking downtown Frankfort. Over the years the school's name changed from the State Normal School for Colored Persons (1886), to Kentucky Normal and Industrial Institute (1902), Kentucky State Industrial College for Negroes (1926), Kentucky State College for Negroes (1938), Kentucky State College (1952), and finally, Kentucky State University (1972). Today, the campus exceeds 300 acres and is the hub of post-secondary education in Frankfort.

Mayo-Underwood football team, down on the Sandbar playground, ca. 1948–49. Front row: Vincent Warren, John Guy, Harold Hogan, Harold Williams, and unknown; back row: Ronald Hansford, Robert Hogan, Clark Roberts, and Leonard Green.

Contributed by Edna Rawlings Washington

Wesley Marshall

Mason Burton: *You mentioned the Sandbar. What was the Sandbar?*

Marshall: *That was down there where the river is. Yeah, that was our football field, and we played baseball down there and basketball. Then, they started putting bleachers down there when we had ballgames. But most of the time when we went on the Sandbar we always went over to the riverbank to fish and other things.*

Barbara White

The Sandbar was a place where everybody gathered. They'd have baseball games down there. We'd just go down there just to play,…and we'd play bound ball and Miss Mary C. Holmes was the director. We would play volley ball. We had to play in the sand or we had crafts. She kept us busy.… We'd just go down there and just have a good time. We'd pack lunches to take down there. When the guys played baseball down there, you know, they had a real crowd.

John Sykes

The Sandbar did flood every year, every time the river would come up. But it was right at the end of Mero Street. Mero Street ran, it was right behind the school. The back of the school was on Wilkinson. So, it was right dead behind the school and it was probably about, I bet it wasn't a hundred yards long.

44

And it wasn't a hundred yards deep, because the older guys used to knock the ball up side the school all the time, across the road. I'd say it was right on the river bank.

William Washington

Mason Burton: *Tell me about the neighborhood; what you and your friends did over there in North Frankfort.*

Washington: *I played a lot of basketball. We'd take a basketball over to what was called the Sandbar—right behind Mayo-Underwood—and we did most of our playing over to—the Salvation Army—basketball. Then, when we got in junior high and high school, we started playing at Good Shepherd's School—we started playing up there. Mostly it was basketball; it was football.*

Well, we played marbles; we'd hang on the block. There used to be a restaurant down on the end [corner] of Mero-Washington Street called Tiger Inn—and we would hang there—hang outside and talk or whatever. Like kids hang around the parking lots today; we didn't have that—like Tigers Inn and one across the street called Shineboy's right on the corner.

Mason Burton: *Tell me about those two places. Did you go in them very much?*

Washington: *Well, I didn't go in until I got to be maybe a junior or senior in high school—we didn't go in 'cause the man who ran it would run us away; it was kind'a like a community family. If you were doing something you shouldn't be doing they would run you out—not like today.*

Mason Burton: *Did you find that kids were very respectful—mindful of adults back then?*

Washington: *They were—very; anybody on the street or anybody in the neighborhood or in church circles, they tell you to do something, you'd just do it 'cause you know you were going to get something when you got home 'cause they'd call....*

James "Papa Jazz" Berry, Charles "Newt" Berry, Margaret Berry, Charles Combs, Robert Redding, and Alonzo Graham at Tigers Inn Restaurant, located on the corner of Mero and Washington Streets, ca. 1960s.

Contributed by Bernice Combs

Marlene Harris Tyler, Charles Finch, and Lee Charles Harris in front of LaVilla Restaurant, a popular spot for high-school and college students, October 22, 1952. The restaurant, located on Douglas and College Streets, was owned by Dr. Eugene D. Raines, chair of the chemistry department at Kentucky State.

Contributed by Grace T. Harris

Ellsworth Marshall Jr.

Marshall: *After the games, we would go to Tigers Inn. Ewing Atkins owned Tigers Inn.*

Wallace: *Can you sort of describe what it looked like?*

Marshall: *It was just a small restaurant…only just a half a block from the school….
Well, mostly where all of the school kids hung out was Tigers Inn. And you wouldn't called that a honky-tonk, because you couldn't do anything but play the Victrola and eat. That's all, because Atkins didn't have anything else except that.*

John Sykes

Sykes: *And let's see, old Ewing Atkins. Mr. Atkins ran Tigers Inn and that's where the kids hung out when school was out and lunchtime and in the evening. Especially in the winter time, that was a teenage joint. That was the only place, about the only place we had we could go.*

Boyd: *What was it like inside?*

Sykes: *Oh, small with a couple of pinball machines and a few booths where we had our*

46

names all carved over the wall. Just like a regular, regular teenage joint, except it was home. Didn't nobody smoke too much then. It wasn't smoky. It was dark in there. The lights just didn't put out like they do now, so it was dark. And we would go in there and meet our little friends in there and drink soda pop. I think that's all he had in there.

Boyd: *When were you too old for Tigers Inn?*

Sykes: *I would say…I even hung out some after I got out of high school, but about the time I got out of high school. I was leaving town anyway. When you get old enough to drive, you can go other places. And when you find a friend that's got a car.*

James Calhoun

All of us worked together. We went together to help. We were a family. We were raised to help each other.... We didn't have much but we were a happy family. Everybody did something. We washed, ironed, cooked. I've got eight brothers...everybody could cook.

Standing: George Letcher, son Jerry Letcher, wife Lina Letcher, Martha Wilson Johnson, Grace Johnson; seated: Arthur Johnson, John Frank Johnson, dog, Steven Blackburn Johnson.

Contributed by Anna J. Samuels

"HE AIN'T HEAVY"

• FAMILY •

"What money can't buy and the law can't limit."
A Slave Ancestor's Wit and Wisdom

TAP THE MEMORIES of Black family members and get them to talking about unforgettable moments from their family's past, then prepare yourself to be deluged by the complexities, contradictions, and commitments of universal family life that come gushing out. The message is clear—the Black family has persevered as perhaps the most beloved institution of the community. Through economic and other hardships, it has been, and continues to be, a sustaining, nurturing force and a source of hope, pride, and belonging.

Frequent and well-attended family reunions offer testimony to the enduring nature of the Black family and the importance of kinship ties. Examples of this are the annual Warren and Metcalf family reunions that draw relatives from all over the country back to Frankfort, the family home. Go to one of these events and you will find a multitude composed of mothers, fathers, grandparents, aunts, uncles, nieces, nephews, and cousins, and cousins, and more cousins—all seeking to reconnect with their Frankfort homeplace and with each other.

Today, in spite of this modern era in which families tend to be smaller and more dispersed geographically, continuity of family ties and an enduring tendency of African American families to ban together produces strong support systems for siblings in a single family or for generations of a family. Yet, families were not, and are not, confined by biological or legal boundaries. A "kin network" defined belonging, but the family door has always been open for "kith" as well as kin. Historically, extended family members were called "Brother" or "Sister" or "Aunt" and "Uncle" even when there was no blood or marital relationship. A brother (meaning any of these) was never too heavy to support. In times of hardship someone was always

49

there to lessen the burden—financial, social, physical, or whatever. Sometimes the support most appreciated was for spiritual uplifting to assist with the demoralization that often accompanies minority status.

Large families such as the Barnetts, Joneses, or Combs, by virtue of their numbers, were quite visible in the community. In addition, families were often multigenerational. The presence of grandparents and great aunts and uncles in the home, or nearby, promoted unity and strength. As caregivers for children with working parents, these older relatives were both "spoilers" and disciplinarians. Extensive family ties wrapped beyond individual nuclear families to envelop other family units. Sometimes it was hard to tell where kinship ended. Thus, even today, when folks jokingly caution you about gossiping, you had better take it seriously. That's because if you are talking to a Davis, you could also be talking to a Clay. If you are talking to a Mason, chances are you also are talking to a Fields. If you are talking to a Harvey, you might also be talking to a Marshall. One thing is for sure—family members might talk *about* each other among themselves, but no one outside the family has that privilege.

At one time geography also helped promote family unity, as many family members lived in close proximity to each other. Yet a common "homeplace" as the nexus of the family was typical. This was the hub, the message center, the touchstone or point of contact for members of large families to stop by and orient themselves to the whereabouts and activities of other family members.

Regardless of the size of the family, shared memories and family traditions unite kin. Families were, and remain, loyal and resilient. Everyday activities such as eating together at meal times or watching television (or in earlier times, listening to the radio) together help create shared experiences and memories that tie people together emotionally and spiritually.

And in the past, given the size of many of the homes, families were by necessity communal. In many homes privacy for family members was a luxury. Rare was the home where each family member had his or her own room. As one person put it, at nighttime the rollaway beds came out and every room in the house became a bedroom. Van Warren remembers trying to beat his cousin John [Warren] home on weekends to get the last vacant bed. Moreover, family occasions involving life cycle events such as weddings, funerals, anniversaries, birthday gatherings, graduations, baptisms, and reunions continue to reunite kin and help create shared memories that strengthen relationships among all the individuals and households that compose the families.

Family identity also served as, and remains, a badge of pride. The family surname was not only a label, but also a source of identity. In the past, particular talents were stereotypically associated with certain families. For example, the Whites (June and Emma), the Chisleys (George and Mildred), the Williamses (Robert and Anna Belle) and the Millions (Alfred and Nannie), among others, were known for their musical talents. Likewise, the Davises, Joneses, and Washingtons were known for their athletic ability. For the most part, the pride in being associated with a specific family strengthened the family unit and motivated youth to achieve. Regardless of what anyone else thought, there was a certain pride in being a part of a particular clan.

Picnics and family outings have been favorite forms of family fun. Sometimes families settled for gathering in the backyard with friends and family, and sometimes they would fix baskets of delicious food, pile into the few cars available, and take off for a nearby park. Some South Frankfort families looked forward to Sunday after-church fishing picnics, when one family with a truck would fill its bed with straw, relatives, and neighbor families and take off to a favorite fishing hole for a picnic. Playing, feasting, and fun filled the remaining daylight hours.

Black families have readily adapted to changing circumstances, whether it be the addition of babies or older relatives to an already-crowded house, a broken family circle caused by death, a broken home resulting from divorce, the loss of family income because of unemployment, or the destructive forces of a bout with Mother Nature. Nothing illustrates this more than the floods that came periodically to the "Kentucky River City" that required families to call upon every kind of support the family could muster. Margaret Berry's memory leads us through one of these harrowing family experiences:

> As far as household stuff, we didn't have no whole lot of stuff to amount to anything, but we lost just about all of it. We had to get out; we managed to walk out [1937], but my mother was going to stay. So the boys had to pick her up and bring her out.... It was home...and everybody would go together and clean up one home, dry it out so they could come in, and then them people would come and help you.... It was a sad situation, but we got together. We laughed and we cried, and it was that good old unity.

Frankfort's African American fathers and husbands have served as breadwinners, role models, and buffers between their families and a sometimes hostile world. For instance, Samuel Hampton (Hamp) Jones was the father of seventeen children. While his wife Martha, mother of the youngest thirteen of his children, tended to the home, he kept his family fed and clothed by working at the Model Laundry, in tobacco fields, and utilizing his talents for wall papering and painting on the side. Yet, he still had time for community activities and was a deacon and outstanding member of Corinthian Baptist Church. The example of responsibility and commitment to family and church that he passed on to his children is evident in the scores of grandchildren, great-grandchildren and great-great-grandchildren who carry on his legacy. But that model is more typical than not of fathers in the community, and hundreds of others could easily have been cited as an example.

Strong women also operated as "family sustainers," as they have from the beginning of their days in this land. And why not? In most cases their "parenting skills" were developed while taking care of two families — a white one and their own. They became the holders of the family secrets, of the fears and failures, and the "keeper of the flame" of hopes and aspirations. Women inspired their families and others and endowed them with pride, loyalty, the spirit of giving, and courage.

51

Historically the Black family has been characterized as multigenerational, loyal, resilient, communal, and adaptive. It is still so today. Listen as older virtues find modern voices. William Washington, born in Frankfort at the end of the 1930s, a graduate of both Mayo-Underwood High School and Kentucky State, was asked why he returned every year for his high-school reunion and why he chose to remain in his present home of Purcellville, Virginia. Probably without even realizing it, his response paid a fitting tribute to his family, his extended family, and to all families that call Frankfort home. He came back for his high-school reunions "just to keep those ties going. I didn't want to lose that family-like atmosphere," and he lived in Purcellville because it "reminded me of Frankfort."

Clarence Williams

Boyd: *What did you do after Mayo-Underwood?*

Williams: *Had a young lady and she was real sweet. But I knew that Uncle Sam was getting after me. I read in the paper and heard on the radio, said, married men are not called in. She didn't know this, so I got to thinking. Said, "I'm going to ask Evelyn to marry me."*

So, we was on a bus, going to a football game. I said, "Evelyn?" She said, "Yes?" I said, "Will you marry me?" "Yes." Scared me, so quick. I thought I'd get a rebuttal.... "I gotta ask my mama."... Then I choked. So, she said, "When you going?" I said, "Well, we can go down like we're going to a speech tournament." And we took her sister with us.

So, we get to Louisville and a cab comes up, and he said, "Where are you going?" I said, "Over to Indiana." "Are you going to jump the broom handle?"... So, we went over there and went into the Justice of the Peace...he said, "Well we got to have a third person, go out there and get the cab driver and bring him in here." Okay, brought him in there for a witness. And my sister-in-law act[ed] as flower girl. So he gave us the vows, told us, "You're married now."

So we came back to Frankfort. She stayed at her house and I stayed at my house, a block apart.... So, fortunately for me, I just happened to be working in Scott's Furniture Store.... My auntie was gracious enough to let me rent her duplex on the side. She didn't ask me if I was married, if I was leaving home or nothing. She didn't say nothing. So that night we went over to Scott's. We picked out our furniture, three rooms of furniture, brand new furniture....

So, it went on and the "beatinest" part about the whole situation, when I got ready to leave my mother, she said, "Where you going?" I said, "Home." She said, "You're already home." I said, "Mama, I'm married." She said, "What?" She said, "Al's gone, and Richard's gone and you're going!" She didn't like that. But everything worked out all right.

Boyd: *What did Evelyn's parents say?*

Williams: *I went to see my dad-in-law. She already told her mother. I give him the certificate. "When did this happen?" I told him. He said, "I think that's nice. I thought you were going to blow it." But we made it through.... And so far we're the parents of four kids, three girls and a boy, grandparents of eight grandchildren and one great one.*

Boyd: *And how long have you been married?*

Williams: *Fifty-four years.*

Anna M. Lindsey Wolfe and Costello Wolfe cut the cake at their wedding, ca. 1945–46.

Contributed by Lillian Barnett

Clarence Williams

Boyd: *Let me ask you about your parents.*

Williams: *They were generous, they were good, they were loving. And Daddy was a cook. Oh man, you give it to him, he'd cook it. Oh, yes. And Mama, she did housework, did ironing, and then she went down in the kitchen with Daddy. Well, Daddy taught me how to do a few things, to make a living.... Our parents are both deceased, but they taught us the right way to do things and the right way to act.*

Boyd: *What were your parents' names?*

Williams: *Frank and Alice Williams.*

Frank Williams and his son, Clarence, sitting on curb in front of 328 East Second Street.

Contributed by Evelyn Williams

53

Five generations: Beatrice Marshall (100 years old), her daughter Moses Railey, her son Frank Williams, her grandson Clarence Williams (Frank's son), and her great-grandchildren, Annette and Clarence Adolph (Clarence's children).

Contributed by Evelyn Williams

James Calhoun

You respected older people. Their word…when they told you something you did it because, if you didn't, when you got home, it was going to be rough. That's the truth.

Clara E. Hogan

Hogan: I grew up almost like an only child and I had four siblings and they were all grown and had children of their own when I was born. So my nieces and nephews are older than I am. I have one six years older, one that's three years older; then I have a nephew that's the same age of me. My brother— I don't know whether you remember—Nelson Turner is 21 years older than me. And so I was sort of spoiled.… My mother and father separated really when I was rather young. I had the brothers and her mother's mother—grandmother; they all raised me and my auntie.… My grandmother's name [was] Charity Dandy and my mother's married name was Fannie Turner; of course, my maiden name was Turner. Corine Graham was a sister and Nelson Turner was my brother and William Henry Turner was my brother and then I had a brother—George Lewis Turner who I never did see 'cause he died when he was seven years old. So that was the extent of the immediate family.

Fannie Turner and granddaughter, Toni Hogan, on Douglas Street, 1952.

Contributed by Clara E. Hogan

54

Barbara White

White: *Mama Sallie,…was my father's mother.*

Boyd: *Sallie Fields?*

White: *Sallie Fields.*

Boyd: *Didn't Sallie have a lot of sisters?*

White: *Yes, Alice King, was a sister. And then she had Annie [White]…she lived in Louisville… then, there was Aunt Cora. I knew three sisters. Aunt Cora, Cora Redd. She lived on Murray Street. And she was, she was a strange lady, because she worked like a man. She did. I never saw Aunt Cora in a dress. She always wore pants. And I mean, she could work. She cut down trees. She helped build a house. There was nothing Aunt Cora wouldn't do.*

The Jones sisters—Alice, Sallie, and Annie (back), and Pearl in front.

Contributed by Cornelia F. Calhoun

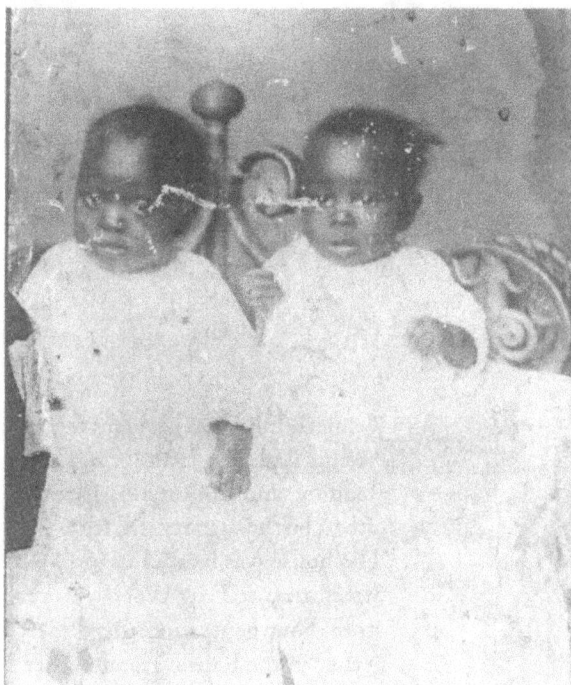

Martha and Mary Jones, twin daughters of Charles and Sallie Thomas Jones. They were born July 3, 1900, and were about six months old when this was taken.

Contributed by Mary E. Clay

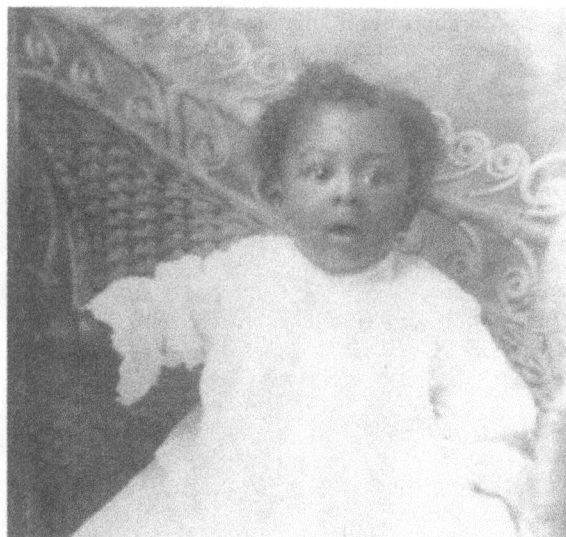

Samuel (Hamp) Jones, age seven months, after his christening, ca. 1915. Jones, father of seventeen children, worked at the Model Laundry for over fifty years and served as a deacon at First Corinthian Baptist Church.

Contributed by Mary Louise Jones Washington

Margaret McIntosh and Lillian Barnett

Boyd: *What did your father do? What was his job?*

Barnett: *Run one of the machines, you know, passing the bottles on that line.*

McIntosh: *Yeah, he did all kinds of jobs.*

Barnett: *And we wore the best clothes in Frankfort, the best shoes and everything, from Meagher's and Capital Fashion. And guess what the kids used to call us? The "Damn" Barnetts...because we had more than what they had. And we'd even take them home and give them supper or lunch, change them, let them wear our clothes.*

McIntosh: *Some were less fortunate than us and there was more of us. I couldn't understand that. And you know, we would help them. But of course, they might have been a one-parent family, too, where we always had a mother and a father.*

Marguerite and Julie Mae McGrapth (sisters), taken on porch in the early 1920s.

Contributed by Elizabeth McGrapth

Kenneth Ellis, Michael Knott, Arthur Redding, John Irving Redding, and Clifton Ellis Jr., after a birthday party, ca. 1958–59. The house was located at 309 Mero Street, next to Frog Wood's grocery store. Four generations lived together in the house: grandmother Maggie Carter Shannon, daughter Mattie Turner, granddaughter Anna Davis, and Maggie's great-grandsons.

Contributed by Dorothy C. McGowan

56

Marjorie Doneghy's first birthday party, 1949. Seated: James Swain, unknown, Frank Brooks Jr., Sheila Mason, Linda Hall; standing: unknown, Linda Williams, Esten Collins, Charlesetta Johnson, Andrew Mason Jr., Marjorie Doneghy, Patricia Hunter, Bernice Williams, Georgia Ann Williams, Clarence Metcalf, Johnny Carson, Wanda Wade, Janice Wade; back row: unknown, Ella Greene, Mike Redd, Dubois Smither, Isaac "June" Greene, Doris Jean Evans, Glenn Douglas, Billy Caldwell, Mike Mason, Phillip Douglas, Mason Harris, Clifton Jones.

Contributed by Marjorie Doneghy

John Sykes

Sykes: *I don't think we even had a fan. So it'd be hot, you know, up to the middle of the night, I'd say around nine, ten o'clock, you'd get that little breeze that would come through there. But before then, you'd almost suffocate. I don't know how Mama stood it. My mother would get up and fix three meals a day. My father worked on the railroad. She'd have his breakfast when he left in the morning, fix lunch for us, and then she'd have his dinner, got dinner when he came home. She cooked over a hot, coal stove.... And how she stood in that little kitchen and cooked, I don't know.*

Boyd: *How many kids were there?*

Sykes: *Later on there was eleven. But I think there was about eight of us then.*

Andrew Mason Jr.'s fifth birthday party in 1952. Esten Collins, Clifton Jones Jr., Martha Patton, Billy Caldwell, Billie Fields, Delores Brown, Anna Delores Coleman, Carroll Lee Martin; in front: Andrew Mason Jr., Sheila Mason.

Contributed by Sheila Mason Burton

Sue Turner and Maggie Knott and other family and friends at a Carter family reunion at the home of Nora Whitney in Green Hill in the early 1950s.

Contributed by Dorothy C. McGowan

Lillian Barnett and Margaret McIntosh

Boyd: *So, how many kids were living in the house at one time?*

Barnett: *Let me see, on Hill Street…the boys slept in the back room. And then we had another room, the oldest sisters would sleep in the second room, then the first room, the youngest girls were sleeping in the first room. Then downstairs…there'd be the back porch and you go in the kitchen door. And there's the kitchen, my Mama and Daddy's room with the old coal stove. The front room with the old grate and everything. And it was a nice front porch.*

McIntosh: *Let me tell you about the bathroom. It was outside.*

Barnett: *Outside.*

McIntosh: *You had to go downstairs and outside. Now, it was called the outhouse, but when you sit down on it, when you get up, the water would flush. That was the only best thing about it.*

Mary Helen Berry

Wallace: *You were pretty young and having to help make it better, to make ends meet….*

Berry: *Well, children had to do that. My brother would deliver clothes for people because all [those who] lived in that area, they did laundry work for the rich white people. And I would go along because my brother, he was oldest, but he was no fighter. I was a fighter. And I had to take up for him when them old bigger boys would take the money from him….*

Millie Combs

Mason Burton: *What did…the little Carter children…do for entertainment out there in Hickman Hill?*

Combs: *The main entertainment was dancing. We all danced to the tunes. We fiddled, old time fiddling, and dancing. Anybody could dance. It was called…old fashioned breakdown.… We didn't have any*

58

parks or anything like that. We didn't have a car or anything, and some of us finally got an old horse and buggy, rode around. We could get somebody to have a old guitar so we could dance, and then finally when we could have a radio, not a radio, but what we call a gramaphone and somebody would carry that around and it was there and everybody danced, young ones and old.

Mason Burton: *Did the whole neighborhood come around?*

Combs: *Oh, yes, and if it wasn't but two or three of them we could dance. Sisters—we had enough sisters that we could dance and go on with our plans and things. We could always get up a nice big party. And my mother always allowed us to bring our company home and have company at home all the time.... They could come to Mama's and eat a meal and stay a day or two. I reckon we would call it a flophouse.*

Margaret McIntosh and Lillian Barnett

Barnett: *And I raised practically all my nieces and nephews. Let me see, the Caldwell family, all of them. And Margaret's kids, three of them, lived right next door. Took care of them while she was working. And Jean [Winkfield], my sister...*

McIntosh: *She's got nine kids.*

Barnett: *Nine, that's right.*

McIntosh: *She got seven girls and two boys.*

Margurite Shauntee

And Kenneth...he went to school and Mrs. Hitch said he gave her his birth date, his name, and then she asked him his father's name, and then he knew it was Frank Shauntee, and she said, "What is your mother's name?" And he said "Mama." And she said, "Yeah, but you say Mama, but she's got a first name. What is her name?" He said "Mama." And she said, "What does your Daddy call her?" He said,

"Honey."

One of Mary K. Robb's birthday celebrations when the family still lived in their house in the "Bottom," ca. 1960s. Jack Robb, Portia Robb, Mary K. Robb, Alice Simpson, and unidentified guest.

Contributed by Margurite Shauntee

59

Dobson family in 1912. Back row center: Beatrice, Lillian, Virgil; second row: Roy, Grandma Annie Dobson, Grandpa Richard Dobson; first row center: Mattie Dobson White at the age of two (born 1910).

Contributed by Edna Rawlings Washington

James Calhoun

Christmas was a big time. We had a big tree we'd go out and get...and we would make ribbons, decorations, ties, we'd get wreaths. We'd go up on the hill and get mistletoe. We would decorate our tree. Mama, she'd make cakes, two or three months before...people had their wine, homemade wine. But there was a big dinner and we celebrated as a family. The neighbors would come in. We'd go to the neighbors' houses. The holiday that was most dearest to you, most times was Christmas and your birthday.

William Calhoun

I remember how Junior [Don Marshall] and Donna [Marshall], how we could go up to their house. When somebody had a birthday party, everybody went to it. You, you just had that kind of spirit. And you were everybody's child. You talk about extended family, yes. Everybody was everybody's child. "I'll give you a whipping" if you, you know.

Charles "Bus" Mason at his favorite pastime, fishing.

Contributed by Billie Mack Johnson

Alice Sanders, Evelyn Williams, Henry Sanders, Sallie Fields, Robert Sanders, and Dorothy Sanders relax in the infield at the Kentucky Derby, in the mid-1950s. Photographed by Clarence Williams.

Contributed by Cornelia F. Calhoun

Margurite Shauntee

My father's people was very close knit, and I know every year, my father and brothers, and some of their friends would go on a fishing trip and they would leave on a Friday...and they would come back on early Sunday morning. And Mr. John Lewis Brooks had a truck...and they would fix it with straw on it and tarpaulin and they would come and get the children and wives and things, and the wives had fixed all these good things to eat, and then we all would go and spend the day fishing.

Mary L. McGee

McGee: *The majority of my youth, I lived on Washington Street, 613 Washington, and we had a real nice childhood. Mother died when I was about ten and my auntie raised me and my sister and brother.*

Mason Burton: *What was your auntie's name?*

McGee: *Nellie Elizabeth Harris. So she raised the three of us after mother died, and she worked hard to raise us and put us through school. She did domestic work at different homes.*

Margaret Marshall, daughter of Charlie and Beatrice Marshall.

Contributed by Cornelia F. Calhoun

61

The Fields and Coleman children with their aunt, ca. 1940s. First row: Anna Delores Coleman; second row: Charles Henry, Mary Evelyn, Cornelia, and Barbara Fields, children of Charles Raymond and Margaret Ellis Fields; third row: Julia Mae McGrapth Ellis.

Contributed by Cornelia F. Calhoun

Sam Parker Sr. and Bertha Parker.
Contributed by Ella Parker Sanders

Bertha Parker, Lizzie, John Offutt Parker in 1908.
Contributed by Ella Parker Sanders

Millie Combs and children—Dorothy, Maggie, Flora Belle, Anna, Geneva, Charles, Mary, Robert, and James—taken after a family gathering in the 1950s.

Contributed by Bernice Combs

Glenn Douglas

Mason Burton: *You mentioned that you had grandparents, tell me what role they played in your life.*

Douglas: *My grandparents…were my disciplinarians, plus they were good, loving grandparents. They spoiled the hell out of us. Excuse the expression. And they raised us good…made me a good person.… I enjoyed being around them. I lived with them…until '54. And, Granddaddy, he was a great guy. I enjoyed my grandfather. I enjoyed my grandmother, too, but my grandfather…never disciplined us. My grandmother, she would do all the disciplinary work. She would spank our butts. Granddaddy, he would just talk to us. I think I remember him spanking us once or twice. That's it. Then he bought us ice cream.*

Josephine Krank

Mother and father, as I remember…he was a student at Kentucky State University—Kentucky State College, I guess it was then—and I think they met at church.… They married while he was here in school, and almost immediately after they married he decided he wanted to leave Frankfort, because there wasn't too much here to do. She wanted to stay with her family. So I think they finally decided that he would go back to Hickman, Ky.—from there he went to East Chicago to work in the steel mills, and he was going to send for her. Now remember, I wasn't even born then, I was in the process of getting here. When he wrote her a letter to come, my mother's sister, Josephine, didn't give it to her. She never did get the letter, and consequently, I was born here without my father here. They just sort of lost connections. So I am a one-parent child.

John Coleman with granddaughter Juanita Brown, and daughter-in-law Loretta Longfoot Brown. Taken at Hickman Hill, ca. 1928.

Contributed by Sheila Mason Burton

Mrs. Georgia Lindsey, known as "Granny," with her great-grandchildren in front of her house on Hill Street, ca. 1958. Standing: Barbara Sanders, Ernest Nash, Alex Sanders III, and Stephen Mason (not a grandchild); seated on porch: Georgia Anne Sanders Nash Raines (granddaughter) and Willard Lindsey (husband).

Contributed by Alex Sanders

Barbara White

My grandparents on my mother's side, Evelyn and Henry Ellis. And we called them "Mama" Evelyn and "Daddy" Henry. Mama Evelyn… did day work. But she was a real force in our lives, because when my mother was at work, she was always checking up on us.… And my grandfather, he was the janitor over at Mayo-Underwood School as long as I was in school. When I went to the kindergarten, we lived right behind the school on Wilkinson Street. And we had the special privilege of going in the back door that none of the other kids could get to go in.

Henry and Evelyn Ellis family reunion, 1961. Seated: Kenneth Ellis, Clifton Ellis Jr., Wayne Fields, Barbara Fields, Debra Harbin, Lois Ellis, Timothy Ellis; second row: Madalyn Ellis, Beverly Ellis, Gary Ellis, ___ Ellis, Dennis Ellis, Bonnie Ellis, Victor Ellis, Lavolia Ellis; third row: Mary Evelyn Ellis, Moses Railey, Ada (Sissy) Ellis, Donna Fields, James Ellis Jr.; fourth row: Patricia (held by Henry Ellis Jr.), Julia Ellis, James Ellis Sr., Margaret Fields (holding Phyllis Fields), Sue Ellis; fifth row: Henry Ellis Sr., Evelyn Ellis, Ada Ellis.

Contributed by Barbara F. White

Willard Lindsey family at their home in the Fort Hill area, ca. 1900. Willard Lindsey, Walter Lindsey, Sister Mary, Mother Mary, Father Willard, Tink Lindsey.

Contributed by Alex Sanders

Millie Combs

We've had a family reunion just about ever since I can remember. That kept the family together.... We just did it...maybe say, "Tomorrow, we gonna have a family reunion. Everybody come on."

Mary Ellis

Fletcher: *What do you remember about your parents?*

Ellis: *They were great workers in the church. My father was a janitor at church and a trustee. He would do most anything. He loved the children.... A loving father—a devoted father. My mother worked too. A strict mother, she was good though. She was blind and she had a lot of ambition about her.*

Mary L. McGee

Mason Burton: *Aunts and uncles have at times been as instrumental, if not more, than parents. Do you still see that happening with our Black families?*

McGee: *Not as much as it did when we were coming up. I don't think as much. In fact, some families are just not close at all, you know, like we were.*

Barbara White

Boyd: *What was it that you learned from your parents and your grandparents that you're now applying, now that you are a parent and a grandparent?*

White: *To be honest. To be stern when you have to be and always feed them good.... I cook every day. My grandkids or somebody is there every day to eat.*

Margurite Shauntee

The Black doctors that worked at Winnie A. Scott…Dr. [C. W.] Anderson and Dr. [E. E.] Underwood, and Dr. [Thackery L.] Berry…Dr. Berry was one of the most outstanding surgeons in Kentucky.

Dr. Edward E. Underwood, physician of the Frankfort community and Kentucky State Normal School, ca. 1930s. Taken in front of Hume Hall at Kentucky State.

Contributed by George E. Mitchell

"I DON'T FEEL NO WAYS TIRED"

◆ EMPLOYMENT ◆

"Think positively and keep busy."

Mary Ellis's Motto

PHOTOGRAPHS AND MEMORIES bring human faces to stories of how Frankfort Blacks toiled for survival in the days of segregation. Restricted employment opportunities created substantial and frustrating obstacles, but diversity of employment within the community did exist. African American entrepreneurs, professionals, and tradesmen exercised their talents alongside farmers, domestics, and day laborers.

A common thread among all the diverse occupations was the pride and dedication with which they approached their daily labor regardless of how menial others may have perceived it to be. Their work products were reflections upon themselves. Thus, the same pride in the medical and dental treatment provided by doctors B. T. Holmes, J. A. Gay, and T. B. Biggerstaff was also characteristic of the laundry work and cooking for white folks by housewives such as Amanda Killerbrew and Mollie Doneghy, who handled starched shirts and other garments and made cakes and country hams as if they were pieces of art.

Work in the African American community was often a family affair. This was particularly true in the rural areas such as Green Hill and Hickman Hill, where farming was the order of day. George Sanders's property on US 60 and that of Harry Clay and Luke Bush in Farmdale were examples of successful Black farms. In the city, as a consequence of restricted employment opportunities, Black households were often two-income households. Although in many cases men were the primary breadwinners, Black women composed a substantial portion of the work-force long before it was common practice for Caucasian women to be employed outside the home. The necessity to support or assist in the support of their families sometimes forced

67

women to turn to neighbors, extended family members, and friends to care for their children while they worked. Those who remained at home often made extra money by taking in laundry, sewing, cooking, or by caring for others' children. Oftentimes by necessity Black youth also assisted in bringing income into the household. Money earned from running errands, delivering groceries, and doing other odds and ends aided in supporting the family, buying clothes and school supplies, and improving family living conditions.

Perhaps the unsung heroes of the Black workforce were the domestic workers. Both men and women left their homes each morning to work in the homes of whites as cooks, chauffeurs, maids, and butlers. For the women in particular, this made for a long day of washing, ironing, cleaning, and cooking for two families—their employers' and their own. To many it was just a job, one that could on occasion have some perks such as gifts of castoff clothing and furniture or surplus food that supplemented cash income. However, sometimes enduring, long-term relationships developed between Blacks and the families who employed them. Clara Hogan remembered playing with the Hanley children on their large farm out near Tierra Linda while her grandma worked in the house. She also recalls hearing her grandma talk of nursing one of the Darnell children and of how kind and helpful Judge John D. Darnell was to her mother when she had to move to a new home to make room for Kentucky State's expansion program. Louise Combs's tribute in *Frankfort Celebration* to Bea Carter Harris, an exemplary domestic, speaks for the Black domestic worker in Frankfort and everywhere: "All the persons she served considered her a blessing and a jewel—kind, gentle, capable, caring person, and sometimes a philosopher."

Domestic workers were often employed by multiple households for set days of the week. The nature of such day work made it possible for many men and women to hold two or three jobs at the same time and, according to Maggie Knott, "make more money working by the day." Margaret Berry's $5.00 per week that she earned from "working sun-up to sun-down, seven days a week" as a domestic left enough to share with her mother, "who was expecting some parts of it" for board.

The work of Black craftsmen and tradesmen is evident around Frankfort today. Some of the homes still standing in South Frankfort were constructed by Lonnie Johnson and Butch Garner. The plumbing in many homes was the work of "Boneyard" Mitchell and the electrical wiring the work of William Stone. Persons constructing houses or restoring older homes sought the services of Sterling Evans, a licensed plasterer. And the stone fence that still separates Briar Cliff Drive from the cliff side was the handiwork of Will Mason, a stonemason.

Though challenged with building a sufficiently large customer base in artificially limited markets, the businesses of Black entrepreneurs during segregation were in abundance in the community. With few exceptions, these Black-owned groceries, bars, barbershops, hair salons, trade shops, and other assorted enterprises were located in the heart of Black neighborhoods. There they doubled as community nerve centers where patrons exchanged gossip, kept up on the news, and fostered friendships. Among the most enduring was the Tiger Inn [colloquially,

Tigers Inn] restaurant in the Bottom, where Mayo-Underwood students gathered on weekdays and Blacks throughout the community gathered at night and on weekends. On the Hill, Howard Green's 40-40 Club was the resident juke joint for years. And a mom and pop grocery store on the corner of Third and Murray first run by the Blackburns, then the Pattons, and then the Masons was a focal point for Blacks in South Frankfort for over four decades. That corner came alive in the evenings as patrons gathered at Spencer's Café, run first by Blanche Spencer and later Jay Spencer, and ending as Calhoun's Café under the ownership of George Calhoun. And finally beauty salons run by Elizabeth Oglesby, Margaret Trowell, and Geraldine Gaines, and barbershops run by Fred Allen, Henry Martin, and Bias Graham pulled in Black clientele from all over Frankfort and Franklin County. The gradual closing of the doors of Black-owned businesses, particularly retail operations, raised questions as to whether the withering of segregation may have resulted in undercutting the customer base of these businesses rather than expanding them.

In addition to Black entrepreneurs, Frankfort had a corps of Black professionals. Certainly teachers and ministers formed the heart of that group. However, at one time at least three Black medical doctors worked at the segregated Winnie A. Scott Hospital: Drs. E. E. Underwood, Charles W. Anderson, and T. L. Berry. Later, Dr. B. T. Holmes provided medical services there alongside a nursing and support staff that included "Grannie" McQueen, Mary Francis Bush, Myrtle Calhoun, and Annie Stepp. Black dentists Dr. J. A. Gay and Dr. T. B. Biggerstaff served the Black community as well as the university. Pharmacists from the People's Pharmacy operated out of the Odd Fellows Hall in the Bottom.

In 1899 Thomas Brooks, Edward Lane, and other prominent men established the first Black newspaper in Frankfort, a weekly named the *Bluegrass Bugle*. Dr. E. E. Underwood became the editor and William Mayo served as a member of the board. The *Bugle* remained in publication until 1918.

A few African Americans found satisfaction in working for other Blacks. James Ellis recalls rewards from "driving for Dr. Underwood," where occasionally his (and Dr. Underwood's) only pay was a good meal prepared by a patient or his family. Other Frankfort Blacks found employment with Earl Tracy's Cab Company or with other Black-owned retail or service businesses in the community. And certainly the employment opportunities at Kentucky State extended beyond what was available on faculty. Still, many Blacks developed loyal careers with white-owned establishments. Several recall the familiar stance of Roberta Wilson at the Grand Theatre movie house. Others remember Anne Graham's work as a seamstress at The Kathryn Shoppe most of her life; Willie Mason, the only Black mechanic at Vaughn's Garage; or J. Todd Simpson in the dining room of the Southern Hotel. Newt Graham and Hogan Hancock were all about town delivering prescriptions for the Fitzgerald Drug Store, and Henry Sanders's face at the Boden Cadillac Car dealership was just as familiar as any of the owners'. Many of these people became more than just employees to the white owners. William Calhoun's dad worked with

Phillip Gordon's One-Hour Cleaners, but he and Phillip sometimes got "cleaned out" together at the racetrack.

Interviews with Frankfort Blacks shed much light on the cultural environment of various jobs. Traditional linkages between class status and occupation existed but may have been somewhat moderated by external circumstances. Segregated housing meant that all economic levels of Blacks coexisted in the same neighborhoods. Thus, professionals resided alongside day laborers and shared common grievances. Moreover, persons holding jobs perceived to be of minimal status could and did serve as community leaders in their churches, social clubs, and civic organizations. Also, climbing the economic ladder for Blacks meant multiple careers for many workers. As employment opportunities in fields formerly off-limits expanded, for many upward mobility entailed possessing the flexibility to change careers on a frequent basis. For example, the Black domestic who became a state janitor and then a state laboratory technician was not an isolated phenomenon.

Black men and women from Frankfort took on the work of "making the world safe for democracy" every time America went to war. One of former KSU President Atwood's favorite stories reflects the reception African Americans received when they came home from military service in World War I. African Americans were not welcomed as war heroes; in fact, Atwood was warned by his father not to appear in public in uniform.

World War II was a tremendous watershed event for Blacks. It was a turning point, a catalyst for change in attitudes and expectations. Black veterans came back from their experiences overseas with heightened expectations for their lives and with the sense that they had earned full citizenship by helping to defeat the forces of fascism. Moreover, expanded job opportunities at northern defense plants meant a number of families left Frankfort for better jobs. If they came back later it was with a different outlook on the type of future that they would be willing to accept. Most of the enlisted men in World War II, like Henry Ellis, who served in both the European and Asian war zones, just "kept hauling supplies and gasoline and everything that went to the front lines" until they were discharged. Veterans such as Maria Qualls, William Isaac Fields, James Graham, and so many others helped win victory in foreign conflict. Younger Blacks, such as Freddie Williams, David Thurman, George Epperson, Ronnie White, Thomas Graves, Eugene Robinson, Glenn Douglas, and Ellsworth Marshall, fought in the steaming jungles of Vietnam. Segregation and job discrimination often awaited African Americans returning from military service. Even higher education did not automatically guarantee special treatment. Equality was something for which Blacks still had to fight, and many African American soldiers grew weary of waging two wars simultaneously. Yet, in spite of occasional discouragements, it was the perseverance of these same Black soldiers that helped bring about victories both on the battlefield and on the home front.

Today, in a different world, one removed from the era of legal segregation, career options for young Blacks exist as never before. Kentucky state government, through programs such as the

Governor's Minority Management Training Program, fosters leadership skills of talented young professionals. Kentucky State University offers bachelor's and advanced master's degree programs to its students. Black physicians, dentists, and attorneys now serve the entire community, as do Black-owned-and-operated businesses. Yet the message is clear: African American leaders, employers, and professionals must, as Mother Ellis noted, "Think positively and keep busy" to ensure that more youth are aware of and take advantage of these greater employment possibilities.

Millie Combs

Mason Burton: *What did people do? Were they mostly farmers or...*

Combs: *They fished and they hunted and sold hides, pelts, and things, and then at that time most men raised cattle and in the wintertime most of the men had jobs round feeding cattle and stuff like that and they raised tobacco and stripped tobacco, things like that.... Nearly everybody raised gardens and most everybody canned and picked blackberries and sold them, or they made stuff for winter.*

Livery, boarding, and feed stable next to Robb and Williams funeral home, ca. 1910s. At the time shown here, there were enough businesses in the area to support mail pick-up.

Contributed by Margurite Shauntee

Farrier at anvil in his shop.
Contributed by Alex Sanders

Henry Ellis

But nobody is supposed to take care of you. You're supposed to learn how to do on your own. That's what you were taught then. Every afternoon, I was working at the Capital Hotel. I bell-hopped there. I shined shoes there.... I made more money shining shoes there than I did working for the telephone company when I did get a job. I was 14.

Mary Helen Berry

A lot of them were poor and they...well, they scratched for a living. You did anything.... They had distillery jobs. Some of them was porters. They worked in drug stores.

Golden McGrapth pictured with his mules at Green Hill area in the early 1940s. Green Hill Baptist Church in background.

Contributed by Elizabeth McGrapth

Lillian Barnett and Margaret McIntosh

Boyd: *Talk about what your parents did for jobs.*

Barnett: *He worked at Stagg Distillery.*

McIntosh: *Before that he worked at Horn Drug Store and he rode a bicycle, because he never had a [driver's] license. And he would go around the neighborhood and deliver the medicine. He always worked.*

Margurite Shauntee

Uncle Jimmy [Johnson]…and my Daddy went there [Schenley's Distillery] and fired boilers at night. And he made more money in one week than some people were making—and so, they all—and Mr. [Albert] Blanton, they were foremen and they had jobs that Black men didn't have in those days.

George Simmons

"Buddy" Ellis used to drive Dr. [E. E.] Underwood around. You could always tell where Dr. Underwood was…because you could see his car out front and "Buddy" Ellis was in the car waiting for him.

James "Buddy" Ellis

Wallace: *What was your first job that you took?*

Ellis: *First job? Well I'll tell you. Let me see. I drove for Dr. Underwood…that's the first job I ever had.*

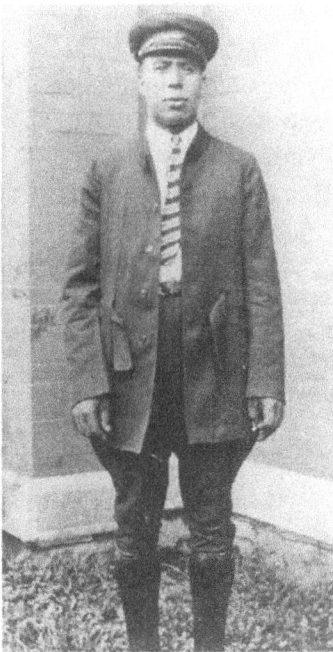

Robert "Dude" Turner worked as a chauffeur for Silas Mason.

Contributed by Mary E. Clay

Mary Coleman, Hickman Hill resident, with one of the children for whom she babysat, ca. 1920.

Contributed by Sheila Mason Burton

Narcissus Clay, who worked as a nurse for the Hoge family in Jett, Ky. (formerly known as Hoge's Station). Later, she worked for the Strassners in Frankfort.

Contributed by Mattie Davis

Henry Sanders

I tell you…the reason I left home as fast as I did, because I didn't like farming.… My uncle Earl Tracy, he had a taxi business…and I had just began to learn how to drive and…I was thrilled to death to drive a taxi.

Millie Combs

I used to work for a place where they had three or four beds and a bath up there, and it wasn't some old raggedy cots…, but you never knew who was coming down out of there mornings for breakfast. I have cooked for them.

Emma Jones Turner and Robert "Dude" Turner, taken at Duntreath Farm in Lexington, where he worked as chauffeur and she worked as maid.

Contributed by Henrietta Gill

Mary Helen Berry

My mother would work for the Averills…and my mother, since she was a good cook, she started making bread and things, and I had to peddle them. And all of my customers were white people. When they [would] say, "Little girl, who made this?" I said, "My mother." "Well, who is your mother?" I said, "She works for Mr. Marvin Averill." That's all I would have to say and, boy, when the food was all over, that's the way my mother dressed my brother and I, and that's why we was able to live better, selling that bread.

Mary L. McGee

The majority of my work was in the private home, and [in] each one of them I worked with children, and every time I'd go with these children I could always remember something that Ms. [Alice] Samuels taught us: "I don't care what kind of occupation you choose, just be the best in what you do." And I think I have done that, because the majority of the children that I brought up are now grown, but they still have time to come by and thank me for the teachings that I gave them.… We ended up being more friends than employer and employee.… I remember one incident, we went to the store, me and one of the girls in the [Jack] Kennedy family, and the lady said, "Honey, your hair is simply beautiful. Who fixes your hair like that?" And she says, "My Mommy does." And she looked at me and said, "Don't you, Mommy?" Well, it was really funny. The lady wanted to say something, but I know for ten or fifteen years, that child called me "Mommy," because I was there every day, five days a week, and to her I was Mommy.… They do become a part of you. And, if you've got a good kid, regardless of color or anything, you gonna love them. And if you're nice to them, they gonna love you.

Dollie Beatty, who worked as a maid, pictured on Blanton Street in the 1930s–40s.

Contributed by Barbara F. White

Georgia Lindsey and Armour Blackburn, ca. 1925. They worked for Pruitt Graham as domestics.

Contributed by Alex Sanders

George Simmons and Henry Sanders

Simmons: *The white people used to come down there and bring their laundry on Monday. And the Black people knew what time to expect them. They would drive up and honk their horns and…the Blacks would go out and get their laundry. They'd come back by the same token and honk the horn, and they'd bring the laundry out.*

Sanders: *They was about half afraid…they'd heard so many rumors about the Bottom.*

Margaret Berry

She [mother] done washing and ironing. And, then, she worked for Jesse O'Dell. And she worked at the home. My mother worked there and cooked and cleaned up for them.

Mary Jones Fleming worked as a cook in the late 1960s. This photo was taken in the kitchen of the Lloyd Robinson family on Seminole Trail.

Contributed by Mary E. Clay

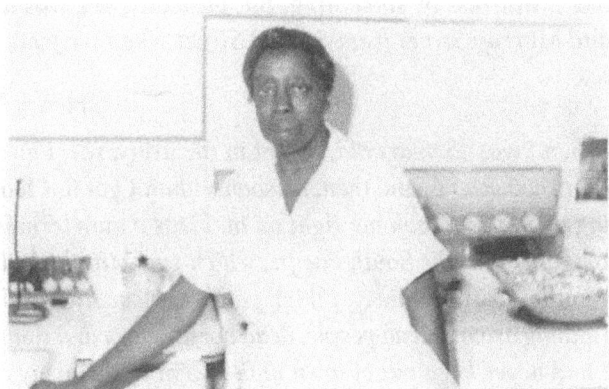

75

Mary Helen Berry

Berry: Most of the mothers had to work and, especially, unwed mothers. Yes, people worked. They either worked out as a cook or laundry workers.... You either was a cook, or you were a nanny, or you did laundry work....

Wallace: Well, you told me a story...about...Mama would bring home food.

Berry: Yes. We called it smother boxes...leftovers...from the table or the kitchen that they didn't want to eat or, if it was enough, they would allow her to bring...because they knew she had children...just enough to feed the children.

Mary L. McGee

Mason Burton: Let me ask you a little bit about what it was like being Black and obtaining the necessities that you needed. What were job opportunities like during your life span?

McGee: Well, the majority of the jobs were babysitting during my time. Now, and it wasn't too many Blacks that worked for the state during my time. I think that has, you know, just opened up lately. Well, I won't say lately, really after all the marches, that's when that opened up where they would have to have some Blacks in each department, but it—when I was young, I don't know of anybody that worked for the state.

Barbara White

My father...worked at Blue Bonnet.... First he worked over at Pete's Corner. And he worked over there for years. And he made ice cream.... He was working for Blue Bonnet out here on Louisville Road, when he passed. But he was a strong man. He wasn't a very big man, but he worked. I never known a time when he didn't work. Even when he was sick, he worked.

And my mother, she worked in restaurants. She was a cook. And she worked in the Knotty Pine down on Main Street. And she worked out at a restaurant out in Jett.... She worked at restaurants all of her life, until she had to retire...but they worked and provided for us.

William Calhoun

Mason Burton: And what about your mom? Was she a stay-at-home mom?

Calhoun: Yeah, pretty much so. She did work sometimes as a licensed nurse, practical nurse for the Winnie A. Scott Memorial Hospital. Mom would work at some times and then, of course, she did some, I guess, child services, you know, for whites throughout. You know, that kind of stuff. She used to work like a waitress or something. But basically, she was a housewife, raising us when we moved to Third and Murray Street from Second Street when we were quite young.

Henry Ellis

When I was 18 years old, I went in the army, see. I got two deferments...when I was in school and...until I finished school, and then, no sooner than I got it, I looked back and they was right there at the door waiting on me, and took me right on in. I was a quartermaster. I went to England, France, Germany, and Belgium, and the South Pacific, which was Manila.... I would haul supplies and gasoline, everything that went to the front line.... I'll tell you how close I was behind the fighting. I'd go through these little towns... running around dead people, dead horses, dogs and things in the road. Right now, it seems like a dream...and I had never been out of town until I went in the army and, then, I...came right on back to Frankfort here.

James Ellis

Wallace: *When you went into the service, you were in the marines.… Did you volunteer or were you drafted?*

Ellis: *Well, then the draft was on and, you go down to Louisville. They examine you, and I forget how many of us went down there that day. Oh, you know, white and Black…we all together went down, singing.… Oh, we was singing on the bus until we got near Louisville. As we was getting near that draft board, everything got just as quiet, you could hear a pin fall. And I remember just as plain, when we was going through there and I was looking on my list and…this guy [said], "Is James Ellis Jr. in here?" And I said, "Yeah, yeah." "Come up here."… He looked at me. He took that stethoscope and listened. He said, "I've got some bad news to tell you.…" He said, "That means you're fit. You can go." He said, "When you go down there, any branch down there you want to join, you can join. They're all going to be after you." And when the marines come out there with all of that dress blue on…that suit got me.… Lord, Lord, I wished to the devil I could find that letter I wrote back to my wife.… I wrote that letter.… Senator Cooper was a good friend of ours, see, the family. And I said…"You see if you can write Senator Cooper and tell him. He's got power in Washington. See how much power he's got to get me out of this damn thing. These fools are crazy."*

Group portrait, World War I, June 22, 1918. Bottom row: Jack Robb with drum, Marcellus Williams; second row: Dude Hunter, Sam Martin, Caroll Chisley, Armour Blackburn, Professor Hayes, Russell Childs, Stewart Henry, George Mason; third row: unknown, Joe Smith, John Morgan Brown, Charles Chisley, Robert Booker, unknown, Frank Campbell; fourth row: Ed Conley, Thomas Washington, unknown, John Woodson, James Henry, ____ Green, Fred Simpson, George Childs, Irvin Childs, unknown, unknown, James "Squeezer" Brown, unknown, Allie Brown, James Scott Ellis Sr.

Contributed by Mary E. Ellis

Robert Garner in World War I
uniform, 1918.

Contributed by Mattie Davis

Glenn Douglas

My dad was, as far as I remember—they were divorced when I was five—he was in the navy for awhile. Then when he got out of the navy, I think he went to work for the state.

James Calhoun

[World War II]…was a turning point.… You would have been living in that…same rut.… It opened up a lot of things, I really think.

Glenn Douglas

I joined the air force in 1962.… Then I, went…to San Antonio, Texas. That's where I did my basic training. And from San Antonio, Texas, I went to Amarillo, Texas. From Amarillo, Texas, I went to Michigan, where I reside now and have been ever since.… I got out of the air force in November 1966. I spent a year in Vietnam.

Carlton Ellis in U.S. Navy uniform
during World War I.

Contributed by Barbara F. White

Harold Williams with friend in the army. This picture was taken
when Blacks and whites were segregated.

Contributed by Evelyn Williams

78

George Lee Harris, bartender at the Knotty Pine Restaurant on East Main Street, 1941. The restaurant was near the electric and water office.

Contributed by Grace T. Harris

George Lee Harris, discharged from the U.S. Navy in 1945.

Contributed by Grace T. Harris

James Basey in his U.S. Army uniform, ca. 1945. Basey was in the U.S. Army from 1944 to 1946.

Contributed by Robert Basey

George Graham playing a banjola, when he was stationed in Jamaica in 1950.

Contributed by Dorothy C. McGowan

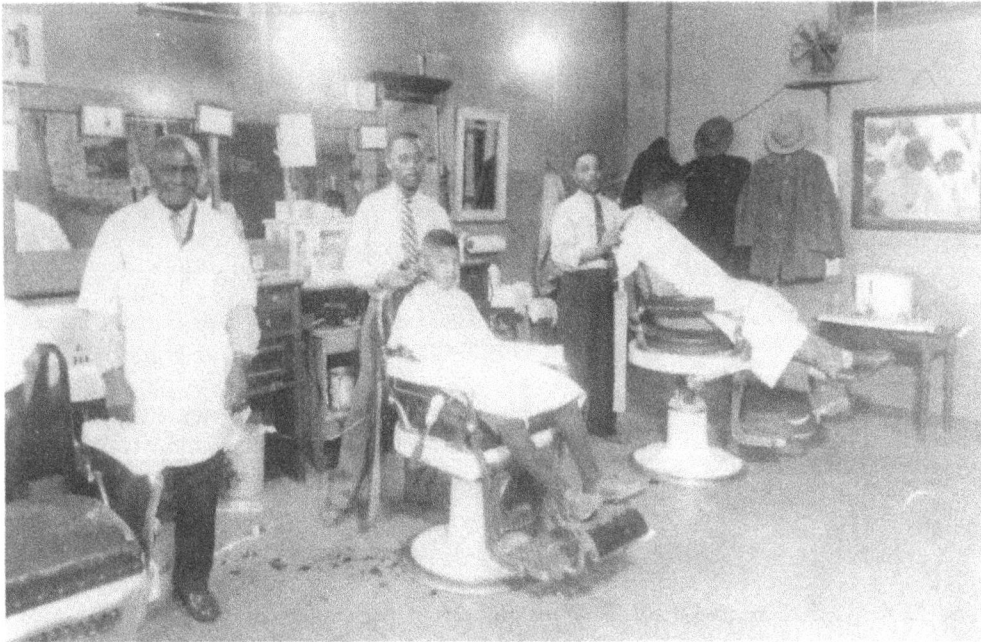

Fred Allen's Barbershop on Clinton Street, in what was then known as Craw or the Bottom. Fred Allen (standing alone), Nelson Morton, and Bias Graham (cutting hair) are shown.

Contributed by Dorothy G. Jones

Archie Surratt

Fletcher: *Do you remember any of the businesses other than the barbershop that was down there?*

Surratt: *Mrs. Oglesby had a beauty parlor—there on Clinton Street. Called "Elizabeth's Beauty Parlor."*

James Graham

And there was...three barbershops, three Black barbershops. You had Bob Martin. You had John Davis, and, then, of course, you had Mr. Fred Allen. And Wesley Martin's father, and there was...the other fellow ...we called him "Corn Puddin.'" His name was Charles Chiles.

Josephine Krank

When I finished Kentucky State in '37, I went to Virginia to teach. And when I came back, I did a lot of different kinds of things. I worked in Blackburn's grocery for some time.... When the war was over I decided I had to find something to do, so I went to beauty school...in Louisville—the Madame Walker Beauty School—and that's how I came to be a beautician. I worked in Elizabeth's Beauty Shop.

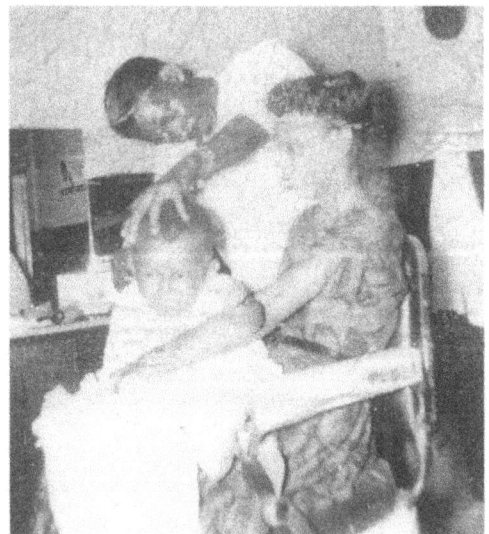

John Davis, local barber, cutting the hair of young Tom Graham (who is held by his mother, Catherine Graham).

Contributed by Mattie Davis

80

Cora and James Scott, who lived on Mero Street across from the Mayo-Underwood High School. Cora worked for the Taylors, who lived on Wilkinson and Main. James cooked at the boarding home on Shelby and Fourth Streets during the 1960s.

Contributed by Cornelia F. Calhoun

Lillian Barnett

Well, I worked as help down to the Tigers Inn after I got out of school. And that lasted about a year. And then after that, started babysitting for the Joe Yagels. Raised all of his kids, when they was small, when they was actually on Beechwood. And then another couple, the Wisemans, helped to raise their kids. And then there used to be an old person's home over on Third Street. That little house that used to be on the corner? That used to be a nursing home, you know, for old people, and I'd go over there and clean up and everything. Then after that, up here, down on Douglas Avenue, where I used to live at, I would baby sit. I practically raised every baby in Frankfort, Black and white.

Maggie Knott

Wallace: What kind of employment opportunities would have been open to you?

Knott: Nothing, but more day work. That's all we could do. That's all we did then. Day work. We'd go somewhere and clean somebody's house and iron for them or something like that, you know. Well, anyway, you'd be making money.

James Calhoun

During that time it was restaurants, white restaurants and Black restaurants. I'll bet you it was at least five white restaurants on Wilkinson, Clinton, the Bottom, and maybe ten Black. Everybody made money. Everybody made money. Everybody had something, big bowls of beans was probably a dime. A piece of cornbread or a muffin, a nickel. Well, they'd give you a big bowl. You'd get full off of that and a bottle of pop or something like that.

Andrew Mason Sr., shown here in 1950, was a bartender at the VFW Post 4075 for several years.

Contributed by Sheila Mason Burton

Workers at the Frankfort State Hospital and School. First row: kneeling—unknown, Friday Walker, Amon Black, standing—Craig Davis; second row: standing—unknown, Evelyn Watson, Henry Mack, Ruby Handy, unknown, Edna Hogan Washington, Alice Sanders King.

Contributed by Barbara F. White

Mary Ellis

Fletcher: *What kind of business did they have?*

Ellis: *They were doctors, dentists, and owned stores and restaurants, cab hauling, and everything.*

James Calhoun

Some of our best educators have come out of the Bottom. I'm thinking of Alice Samuels. She was principal of Mayo-Underwood School at one time and she was a teacher, school teacher.... In that area...we had doctors, lawyers.... I mean, it was a thriving area.

Mary Ellis

Fletcher: *What did most of those people do to survive?*

Ellis: *Cooking.*

Fletcher: *What about the men? What did they do?*

Ellis: *They worked around the farm, whatever they could find to do. Later years...those young guys were bricklayers.*

Clara E. Hogan

Fletcher: *What kinds of jobs were Black men and women doing? You talked a little bit about the women working in the homes.*

Adell Mason and a Stewart Home School administrator, taken at the school. Mrs. Mason was cook at the school.

Contributed by Andrew Mason Sr.

82

Dudley "Dud" Samuels, Margaret Merchant, Doug "Dee" Samuels, Pearl Creal, and Birdie Samuels [White] of Samuels Catering provide refreshments for an event.

Contributed by Ora Mae Cheaney

Hogan: *That was mostly all they could do at that particular time; now when we graduated from high school, we couldn't go into the state office buildings at that time as secretaries, clerks, or what have you. The only thing you could do was to go into white people's homes and clean house or do the laundry work or baby-sit; a lot of baby sitting was going on 'cause I did a lot of baby sitting.... That was just about the extent of domestic work for the women. And then—men, 'course they were janitors.... The state did hire them—and the banks, merchants to clean the stores—and delivery, like drug stores and grocery stores.... 'Course mostly all my husband did was stone work.*

W. C. Jacobs Jr., W. C. Jacobs Sr., and Robert "Bob" Hogan at work in the 1960s.

Contributed by Clara E. Hogan

Robert "Bob" Hogan at work in the 1960s.

Contributed by Clara E. Hogan

In-home daycare facility operated by Adell Mason, shown ca. 1972–73. The children in foreground facing camera are Lyris Cunningham and Ju Ju Papailler. Ju Ju became an actor on Sesame Street. The woman at left is a state inspector of daycare facilities.

Contributed by Billie Mack Johnson

Mary Helen Berry

Berry: *I had always wanted to be a stenographer.... I had wanted to be, first, a dancer because I danced for years, ballerina. Because I was very tight-jointed and that's what I wanted to be. Then, I says if I couldn't be that, I would be a stenographer.... My next was a beautician, and I lined it up.*

Wallace: *Who taught you how to do that?*

Berry: *My mama. I saw how she fixed my hair and I learned to do it and, then, the kids would trust me and, then, I...was making money. And we laugh about it now. I said...was a curl called twist curl, we'd do that for 15 or 30 cents, and we'd get your hair pressed because you had to wash your own hair, I said, "Man, I wish somebody would come in and ask me to curl their hair, all prissy." For that price...we didn't have no shops, but it wasn't like it is today because there wasn't no licensed beautician. We could just do, because I was a child; going to school, making money.*

James Graham

Well...my mother was a seamstress. She made, actually made our own clothes. Made our clothes every year up until we were about, say, probably 14, 15 years old.... She worked in the home and...when the Kathryn Shoppe was opened Ms. Kathryn Roberts hired her as a seamstress, and she stayed there for 30-some years. Her name was Anne Graham.

George White and Clarence Williams, popular bartenders at several Frankfort events. This photo was taken at the Governor's Mansion, ca. 1980s.

Contributed by Barbara F. White

George Simmons

She used to be a seamstress at the Kathryn Shoppe. I mean everybody Black and white, they would always look to Anne Graham for whatever type of dress or whatever they wanted because Anne knew what they liked and they knew Anne knew.

And when it came in, she'd call them and tell them, "I got something in I think you would like." And when they came in and looked at it, they liked it and if there was anything to be altered on it, Anne did the alteration. And she took more work home with her than she did on the job.

The Alex Sanders family, owners of Tiffs Record Shop, 1976. Alex Sanders Jr., Alex Sanders III, Barbara Sanders, and wife Mae Mason Sanders, seated, in the shop at 571 East Main Street.

Contributed by Alex Sanders

Josephine Krank, first Black civilian supervisor of Kentucky State Police, pictured in 1980.

Contributed by Josephine W. Krank

Margaret McIntosh

Boyd: *Tell me what it was like…cooking for the governor.*

McIntosh: *Well, back then they didn't have the Derby Breakfast on the outside, it was all done on the inside. And we would have to start a month before, cooking the country hams. But the scrambled eggs and cutting up the potatoes and apples, we did that the night before the Derby. Or maybe two nights before the Derby and put them in the refrigerator, where they wouldn't turn dark. And then I've worked over there from six in the morning, until twelve at night. And Governor [A. B.] Chandler…he asked me, he said, "Well, how do you get home at night? You ever here this late?" I said, "Well, I walk." Back then nobody bothered you on the street. They wouldn't dare touch you. And he said, "You walk home? Well, these, excuse the French, these two are sitting here on their 'a,' they can get up and take you home. And I want them to pick you up, too." So, I would come to the Bottom in a state trooper car.*

Boyd: *Well, that means he liked your cooking.*

Barbara White

White: *I became the first woman, African American to hold a state position with the state register for the state of Kentucky.*

Boyd: *Yes, I've heard that. Tell me about that.*

White: *It's just being in the right place at the right time. It really was. I started as a nosologist. My cousin, Shirley [Hogan] hollered at me at a stop sign one day and said, "Barbara go take the nosologist test, you qualify." I didn't even know what a nosologist was, so I went and took the test. And I was hired.… And I worked at the health department.… Went to the Office of Vital Statistics as a nosologist. Okay, from a*

Gov. A. B. Chandler signing proclamation to open Kentucky State Police Force to Negroes before a group of NAACP representatives in 1959. Chandler seated. Standing: unknown (partial face visible), unknown (woman with beads), unknown, W. J. Hodge (man with glasses), Laura Chase, Helen Holmes, Jennie Buckner, Archie Surratt, James Crumlin, Marjorie Hall, Garland Offut, George Simmons.

*Contributed by
Archie L. Surratt*

nosologist, I went in as a nosologist, I got promoted to senior nosologist. And then I went to a nosologist supervisor. Then I went to administrative section supervisor. They needed somebody to fill in for the branch manager, so I said, "Well, I'll fill in for sixty days." Well, I filled in for sixty days and after sixty days was up, Fontaine Banks came down and said, "Would you like this job?"... I thought about it, and thought about it, and then I told him, "Yeah, I think I'll take this job. I think I can handle it," and I did.

Josephine Krank

I started as a clerk in the Auto-Theft division and...sometime during that period I went to Kentucky State and took a course in business.... I became secretary to the head of the auto-theft division...and at that period he was trying to find somebody to supervise the people and so he chose me.

James Calhoun

You went to church. You had Sunday school.... That was a must.

Rev. and Mrs. James Gordon of the First Baptist Church, High and Clinton Streets, during Rev. W. H. Ballew's pastorage (1919–32).

Contributed by George E. Mitchell

"HALLELUJAH ANYHOW!"

◆ RELIGION ◆

"We saw our future in church…church was important.
Church was a part of us…not a burden."

The Rev. William Calhoun

THE CHURCH STANDS AT THE HEART of the Frankfort African American community. Testimonies joyously shared between the "Hallelujahs" and "hand-wavings" on Sunday mornings attest to the Black church as a family place—a place where one can really belong, be accepted and cared about, and can contribute something in return. Obviously, the Black church has always been more than just "church" where one goes on Sunday to fulfill spiritual needs and to find "release," although it has certainly served those needs well over the years.

African American churches have helped sustain a viable Black community. They have initiated many different institutions—orphanages, hospitals, schools, nurseries, libraries, youth groups, recreational centers, and more—to aid in meeting the earthly needs of their congregations. As religious institutions, they are also a unifying force, drawing congregants from households throughout the various Black neighborhoods. The individual churches have long served as a communication network, both within their own congregations and among each other. Moreover, they provided a social welfare network long before such a role was assumed by government. Certainly, this communal spirit pervades the memories shared in this volume's images and oral interviews. That is the spirit still heard and felt in daily conversations of the members and friends of the churches.

As one might expect, the worshippers gathered in the Black churches on Sunday mornings were a mixture that transcended generational lines, economic status, origins of birth, and geographic neighborhoods. Thus, the young and the old, the poor and the well-to-do, the Frankfort born and bred and new arrivals, and those living in North, South, East and rural Frankfort and Franklin County all united on Sunday mornings for a common cause. Members of particular families often dominated the congregations in the rural churches, which tended to be smaller. Thus, one might encounter several members of the Combs and Gaines families on a visit to Green Hill Baptist Church or several members of the Clay, Tracy, and Sanders families on a visit to Little Benson Baptist Church. Membership in the three larger churches in the city was less likely to be dominated by a few families, though certainly family and church associations were common. For example, a strong contingent of the Jacobs, Mitchell, Johnson, or Barnett families was usually present in First Baptist Church each week. Likewise, the Sanders, Chisley, Redding, and Fields families were usually in abundance at Corinthian Baptist Church. One visiting St. John A.M.E. on Sunday morning expected to be greeted by members of the Berry, Robb, or Metcalf families. Still, it was not uncommon for members of the same household to be dedicated members of two different churches, particularly the Methodist and Baptist churches. This "divided but equal loyalty" served to strengthen the ties among all the churches.

Certainly ministers have always ranked among the elite within the Black community. They held positions of power, served as an interface with the white power structure, and at times were viewed as the "voice" of the people. Some of the Baptist ministers spent several years in Frankfort, in contrast to the shorter terms traditional to the Methodist ministers. Yet, length of tenure was not an indicator of influence and impact. The expectations of the times in which they served propelled some into the forefront. For example, the Rev. Edgar Mack, pastor of St. John A.M.E., found himself in the center of the 1960s civil rights struggle alongside KSU students and the NAACP. Mack's incisive, no-nonsense approach in filing the joint suit to integrate the public schools was remembered by A. L. Surratt: "He said he wanted the suit to include [integrating] everything, including the cockroaches!"

Likewise, the Rev. Martin Luther King Jr. looked to a trusted friend and colleague, the Rev. K. L. Moore, pastor of the First Baptist Church, to help organize his historic march on the state capitol in 1964. And the special leadership skills of the Rev. Melvin Hughes of St. John came to the forefront in the aftermath of the 1978 flood, when he coordinated efforts of volunteers like the Mennonites and assisted victims, regardless of their church affiliations, in restoring their homes. Still, some of the most cherished memories of service to the community are of ministers who were not in charge of a particular congregation, but whose ministry enveloped the entire Black community. The Rev. Isaac Greene and his devoted wife Beatrice prayed over many a sick bed in hospitals and homes in the community. And other devoted men of the cloth like the Rev. Flem Tracey, the Rev. W. R. Todd, the Rev. Edward Campbell, and the Rev. W. W. Jones were major sources of inspiration and comfort in the community.

Few Black ministers could survive without talents and jobs outside their calling. Dr. E. E. Underwood was not only a minister, but also a practicing "medicine man" and productive "historian, editor, orator, poet, politician, and withal philanthropist." When the Methodists erected a new church on the corner of Clinton and Lewis Streets, an instructor of mechanical arts from the college served as the designer, and the Rev. J. M. Turner, pastor of the A.M.E. Church, a brick mason, helped execute the project. It seemed natural then that the Rev. Charles E. Cobb would serve for several years concurrently as pastor of St. John A.M.E. and as chaplain at Kentucky State or that the Rev. W. R. Hutchinson would create a way to start a Baptist Student Union in the late 1940s on the college campus at the same time that he attended his flock at First Baptist Church. The Rev. Charles N. King was always active on "the Hill," while at the same time he served Corinthian Baptist Church.

Leadership roles in the churches were also very diverse and not relegated only to those with professional or other leadership roles in the Black community. Persons from the entire social and economic spectrum worked together as Baptist and Methodist deacons, stewards, and trustees to move the churches forward. The same applies to the role of women in leading the churches. As nurturers of the family, women moved naturally into the role of nurturer of the congregations of which they were a part. They came to the churches from all social and economic levels to teach Sunday school, run daycare centers and special programs for children and young adults, conduct workshops and other learning experiences, and to provide pastoral assistance whenever needed—with or without official church titles.

Some of the activities of women resulted in clubs, such as the Believers Club at St. John that was initiated to draw the diversity of talents and experiences into a harmonious working unit. A few churchwomen took on extra-challenging tasks usually completed by men. Mother Jones, who started a small church in a house in the Bottom, was remembered by Henry and Margaret Ellis as "a very special woman" who overcame a church fire and urban renewal. And many in South Frankfort remember the Little Church on Third Street that Mattie (Sis) Brooks operated as a layperson.

The Black church was "a hub of activity for Black children." Those interviewed spoke of Sunday school, Vacation Bible School, Baptist Training Union (BTU), Christmas parties, ice-cream suppers, and candy pulling. Parents welcomed the role of the church in their children's lives because they knew it was not only a safe haven, but also a good training ground for their children's spirituality, talents, and aspirations. Many remembered seeing Alice Samuels, called the "Pied Piper" of First Baptist Church, walking every Sunday with a line of children following her to Sunday school. Others recalled Glenna Robinson and Mama Jenny Metcalf making weekly stops for South Frankfort children and Archie Surratt filling his car to capacity to transport people to Sunday school at the St. John A.M.E. The Vacation Bible Schools at First Baptist and Corinthian attracted children and teens from Black communities throughout the city and county. Unlike current-day Bible schools, these were held in the daytime, generally starting at nine and lasting until afternoon. Sunday evening sessions of BTU at First Baptist were as much social occasions for the youth involved as they were religious meetings for the adults doing the training, and they even attracted a fair share of Methodist youth. And the "Heaven and Hell" socials sponsored by Viola Trimble at St. John A.M.E. Church were popular fundraisers supported by youth throughout the community.

Not to be forgotten is the role of the Salvation Army in the lives of Black youth. Each Sunday afternoon South Frankfort kids would wait on street corners for vans to transport them to the Salvation Army, where they would join with their friends from North Frankfort for J-O-Y, a youth revival-style religious service. And on Thursdays after school the girls would meet at the Salvation Army for Sunbeams and Girl Guards, organizations similar to Brownies and Girl Scouts. All of this culminated each summer with the opportunity to spend a week swimming and singing around a campfire at the Salvation Army camp in Ohio.

Cooperative efforts have a long history among Black churches here. Shortly after the Civil War, when the Little South Benson Church was built, the Methodist and Baptist services shared its sanctuary on alternate Sundays of each month. Revivals, including early ones held under tents on the corner of Second and Murray Streets, were joint church efforts for many years—and a major source of increasing memberships and baptisms for each church. The revivals had even further meaning for many of the young people. Mary McGee's memory speaks succinctly on this:

> I remember when we were in school when we'd have revivals. It would be joint revival where the Methodist, First Baptist, and Corinthian Church would all go together, and the three ministers would come to the school, and we'd all go in the auditorium, and they would talk to us and invite us to the revival...and it made it kind'a nice, you know, the working together.

When urban renewal displaced Corinthian from the Bottom, both the Black and white community answered the church's "Boot Strap Operation" call for help to rebuild. A new church and community building now sit on the corner of Second and Murray under the leadership of the Rev. L. A. Newby.

A spirit of vibrancy permeates the Black religious community today. The three major churches are still very prominent in the city; Green Hill Baptist Church is still thriving as a smaller "rural" church, and other predominantly Black churches such as the Seventh Day Adventist, Bethesda Temple, and the House of God Church-Keith Dominion have been established and have growing congregations. Each year the churches and the university combine forces for a celebration of Martin Luther King's birthday, and the university itself has served as host for Sunday school (and sometimes 11:00 o'clock services) for students, faculty, and others. Freedom of religion ranked among the earliest and most cherished of freedoms among local Black residents; it is still so today.

James Calhoun

People's religion has been [the] one thing in Frankfort, that whatever happened...the churches used to be full. On Sunday...the black man was in church.

Mary Ellis

In those days there wasn't nothing to do but go to church.

Green Hill Baptist Church, Green Hill Lane, East Frankfort. The church was organized in 1892.

Contributed by Edna Rawlings Washington

Green Hill Baptist Church Sunday school class.

Contributed by Elizabeth McGrapth

Rev. Robert Brown and Harriet Thomas Brown, taken on Evergreen Road in front of their home. He was pastor of Little Benson Baptist Church on Evergreen, located diagonally across from the Evergreen Baptist Church. They were the grandparents of Mrs. Lucille Jameson. Harriet Brown died in 1958. The Evergreen Road area is, historically, one of the Black neighborhoods.

Contributed by Lucille Jameson

Maggie Knott

We had a church out at Hickman.… It got so people kept dying out and moving back, you know, away and everything. So there wasn't enough out there to keep the church going. So we merged with St. John down there.

Helen Holmes

I was on the Trustee Board. I was on the Steward Board…I was a constant goer.

Composite of officers of the First Baptist Church, July 1, 1924. Top row: Mrs. S. W. Underwood, Miss N. C. Coleman, Mrs. E. T. Strauss, Rev. W. H. Ballew, pastor, Katie Combs, Mrs. Francis Hocker, Susie Carroll; second row: Branum Graves, John McCann, Nelson Dickerson, Edward Oden Sr.; third row: R. D. Glenn, Dr. C. W. Anderson; fourth row: Richard Redding, John S. Shelton, George B. Moore, George Lowry; fifth row: Henry Clelland, Albert Workins; sixth row: Etta R. Banks, B. B. Combs, Robert Combs, Hallie Beatty; seventh row: Miss E. Collins, Thos. K. Robb, Granville Hawkins, ____ Hall, unknown.

Photo by Cusick. Contributed by Rev. K. L. Moore, pastor First Baptist Church

Green Hill
Baptist Church
Sunday school
class.

*Contributed by
Elizabeth
McGrapth*

Mary L. McGee

Mason Burton: *What role did the churches—I'm talking about all the churches now, Black churches in Frankfort—what role did they play in the lives of Black folks in Frankfort?*

McGee: *I think they played a big role because at that time, the churches worked together. I remember when we were in school when we'd have revival. It would be joint revival where the Methodist [St. John A.M.E.], First Baptist, and Corinthian Church would all go together, and the three ministers would come to school. In the meantime, the teachers had already checked to see who belonged and who didn't belong. And these three ministers would come to church, and we'd all go into the auditorium and they would talk to us and invite us to the revival. And I remember when I accepted Christ I was at the First Baptist Church. In fact, there was about fifteen of us that joined that night and the majority of them that joined went to Corinthian. And, then, you'd have so many nights at each church for this revival. And, at the time, as I said, I was at First Baptist when I joined. I think my sister joined the same time. Sunday, the preacher would read the names of those who joined and what churches they joined, and we had about fifteen the night that we all was at First Baptist, and I imagine that there were about thirty children at the First Baptist between the ages of twelve and sixteen. And, it made it kind of nice, you know, the working together. That's what I'd like to see here again too.*

Mason Burton: *Did the church have any kind of community or social involvement? Were there activities that went on beyond Sunday morning? Was the church involved at times when people had disasters, floods, etc.? Do you remember?*

McGee: *I can remember that Big Flood. I always called [it] the Big Flood of 1937. And the churches helped people, you know to get out, but as far as helping them, you mean financially and all, I don't think they did because they wasn't really able.*

Mary Smith

He [Rev. George White of St. John A.M.E.] had picked up this feeling that the people who lived in town did not feel "welcomed in the same way" or as comfortable as the people who worked at the college or lived in College Park.... Well, that was just hard for me to understand. Well, anyway, the Believers Club was created to do that, and so members, women, who were selected lived downtown and those who lived in College Park, to start a club and it got started.... We planned activities that we thought would help to bring people closer together, and I really do think it has helped a lot in terms of the church.

Kentucky State College Sunday school on Easter, 1945. This was a non-denominational Sunday school and church. Kentucky State had a chaplain, but different ministers would frequently handle services on Sundays. This photo was taken in front of Hume Hall, which was also the site for the Sunday school.
Front row, from left: Sandra Ellis [Davis], Mary Anne Jones, Sandra Carita Wright, Arnold Wood Wright Jr., Jimmy Madison, James H. Manley, Delores Manley, Sue Bradshaw, Raymond Harris, unknown, William Dixon IV; second row: Horace Raines, unknown, Theodore Daly, Adranna Hogan, Mary Belle Brown, Eugene Raines Jr., unknown, unknown, Harold Hogan, Albert Harris; third row: college students, boy in center is Robert Hogan; gentleman in rear is Sunday school superintendent J. H. Ingram.
Photo taken by Dr. J. T. Williams, who was dean of Kentucky State College for Negroes.

Contributed by Lillian Wright

First Baptist convention group, taken in front of the state Capitol in 1941.

Contributed by Harry Craig

Mary Helen Berry

Our first church [First Baptist Church, Clinton St.] was down there behind the prison wall.

Glen Douglas

Douglas: *Church was fun. I enjoyed going to church when I was here.*

Mason Burton: *What church did you go to?*

Douglas: *First Baptist Church. And we attended Sunday school, we attended the main service, the eleven o'clock service. And then we attended BTU at night as a matter of fact. And we enjoyed all of these things. And I sang in the choir. I belonged to all of the kids' organizations. We just had a good time.*

Mason Burton: *Did you ever go to the Vacation Bible Schools that First Baptist used to have?*

Douglas: *Yes…Corinthian Baptist Church too.… Yeah, I remember them. The pastor at the time was Rev. Smither and ah, one of his sons was a friend of mine, Dubois Smither.*

Easter Sunday at Corinthian Baptist on Mero Street in the 1950s. Marsha Williams, Sharon Jones, Delores Fields, Yvonne Martin, and Dorothy Mae Sanders.

Contributed by Cornelia F. Calhoun

97

Rev. Charles N. King with Sunday school at old Corinthian Church, ca. 1960.

Contributed by Evelyn Williams

Last worship at Corinthian Baptist Church, ca. 1960s. Front row: Rev. Charles N. King, Rev. Brady Samuels; back row: Sallie Fields, Alice Sanders, Eva Johnson, Roberta Wilson, Jennie M. Buckner.

Contributed by Evelyn Williams

Ground breaking for Corinthian Baptist Church Fellowship Hall, later known as First Corinthian. Left to right: Mary Lee Hunter, Rev. Charles N. King, Jennie Mae Buckner, Lawrence Roberts, unknown.

Contributed by Cornelia F. Calhoun

Barbara F. White

And in the summer we'd go to Vacation Bible School, because Corinthian Baptist Church was right down the street. It was like two blocks from where we lived. And Mama Sallie, which was my father's mother…Sallie Fields, she went to Corinthian Baptist Church, so we were involved in the Vacation Bible School activities of the church. At six, I joined the apostolic church, and that was the church that was in the Bottom. And Mother Jones was the pastor there, Bethel Temple. I joined that church at six years old and well, we went to revival and they scared us so bad, I joined the church. I didn't know what I was doing. I just said, I'm joining. And Mother Jones was a lady pastor. She baptized me…. And I remember that church. My grandparents were really active in that church.

My mother didn't go to church a lot then. She'd go off and on. My father would go every Sunday, but my mother would go like off and on. But later in life she became, she was reborn, and then that's when she really started going. But she was brought up in the church like her brothers and sisters, but sometimes people kind of stray. But later on then I joined the Corinthian Baptist Church and that's where I'm a member now.

Women's adult Sunday school class of First Baptist Church, in August 1956. First row: Lillie Blackburn, Atha Mitchell, Florence Roberts, and Gladys Hutchison; second row: Cordelia Coleman, Viola Kellis, and Lena Greene; third row: Valoise Pennie, Edna Collins, Sarilda Guy, Daisy Evans, Nora Paine, Catherine Demaree, Mrs. E. B. Blanton, Rev. Hutchison, and Euberta Brown.

Contributed by Josephine W. Krank

K. L. Moore

Boyd: *How would you characterize the role of First Baptist Church in the Black community? What is the function?*

Moore: *Well, the very fact that it's named First, suggests that it was potentially the pattern-setter. The pattern-maker. First, as in the first [Black] Baptist church downtown, denotes a prior status. That's the reason why they call it First. It was the first, it's the oldest. And being the oldest, it has had time to cement certain procedures and certain methodologies.... And this carries over, so that, it also produces a certain kind of competitiveness. You only have so much community, you aspire to lead the community.... I've always felt that there's need for all groups and all groups ought to cooperate so that the main purpose is not neglected.... There's a big fight out there with the devil.*

Boyd: *How would you contrast the style at First Baptist with the other Black churches here in Frankfort?*

Moore: *Similar styles, so that it almost becomes a racial style. There would be less differences between denominational styles in terms of the Black church as compared with the white church.*

Gladys Hutchison

Well, they expected miracles from us then, they did. And it is so interesting to see how things have changed. Like, now a pastor gets a gas allowance. He [Rev. William R. Hutchison Jr.] had a car.... There were no vans then. And this car would go and pick up the Stallards out at Bridgeport. There were some old ladies over in South Frankfort, in a nursing home that a Miss Sarah had or something. He would have two people to go and do that. People had to go to the doctor; they'd call him; he'd go take them. And nobody thought of saying, here's ten cents on your gasoline. But see times have changed now. We paid our own long distance phone calls and now the church is paying everything, even for the newspaper that the minister has.

K. L. Moore

Boyd: *What are some of the things that First Baptist does to interact with the larger community, not just the congregational community?*

Moore: *Well, it participates in community-wide affairs. When they had the*

Children of St. John A.M.E. Church dressed up for a Special Day, ca. 1964. Front row: Juanita Gay Mason, Derrick Brice, Leigh Allen; back row: Deborah Berry, Tanya Graham, Toni Hogan, India Baker, Betty Fletcher, Connie Beckley.

Contributed by Archie L. Surratt

Green Hill Baptist Church congregation and others from Frankfort at appreciation services for Rev. William H. Ballew Sr. at a Baptist church in Louisville, 1959.

Contributed by Dorothy C. McGowan

flood, it did not go by color. It went by condition, so that whomever and wherever need was found, response was made. One of the fine things about Frankfort is, when there is a crisis, distinctions don't matter that much. It is time to assist and to help. And I've never, I've never found it to be otherwise. When we had the integration problems…and Martin King came here, that was a community-wide thing that was held, in which all of the churches participated.

Archie Surratt

Fletcher: *When did you establish your relationship with St. John? When you first came here?*

Surratt: *Didn't start immediately, but less than two months after I got here, I became a member of St. John…actually I was a United Methodist…and [Rev. Charles] Cobb was also our chaplain. And he said to me: "One of these days I thought you were going to come on and join my church. We're going to make this our church." And I said, "I probably will." And he said, "We missed you last Sunday." Well, what I was doing then, I'd go to First Baptist this Sunday, go to Corinthian next Sunday, and then third Sunday, I'd go back to St. John. In the beginning…I was what you'd call a "bench member" at first. Then I got involved with the choir and the Sunday school, and then from there it was just dangerous to get on anything because if you got on it you couldn't get off it.*

Beulah and P. P. Watson, 1973. She was Sunday school superintendent at Corinthian Baptist Church, and he was an ordained deacon. Bea Carter Harris, sister of Rev. P. A. Carter.

Contributed by Cornelia F. Calhoun

Rev. and Mrs. Isaac Greene Sr. and Mary Emma Ellis at an activity at Corinthian Baptist Church, ca. 1980s.

Contributed by Cornelia F. Calhoun

Annual Bible Convention at the Greater Zion Tabernacle Church, August 1983.

Contributed by Barbara F. White

William Washington

Washington: *We attended Corinthian Baptist Church and that was on our side of town, two blocks over from where I lived on Mero, so almost everybody in the neighborhood went to Corinthian. I remember Rev. Smither was there and then Rev. King was the pastor.... I went to Vacation Bible School, Sunday school, and we all went to church every Sunday, you know, and everybody in the neighborhood went to church. I remember when I first joined, an evangelist came here, 1947, or somewhere in that area and a lot of us went up. It was kind'a funny like a chain reaction. Five of us went up and after they saw us, 'cause they thought we were bad, after we went up a couple of them went up and been going to the church ever since.*

Rev. James Todd and Charlotte Davis at Corinthian Baptist Church Sunday morning services after a Mayo-Underwood School reunion held in the 1970s.

Contributed by Josephine W. Krank

Mason Burton: *There were three Black churches in that neighborhood.... Was there much interaction among the churches?*

Washington: *We tried to go, when we were young, we tried to go to one of those churches at least once a month. We'd go like to St. John and First Baptist. Like Sue Bradshaw and that family, they went to the Methodist church—St. John—and so we knew them; they were living on Hill Street, in that area, and we'd try to go with them sometimes. Most people on the South side went to First Baptist, so then we would go up there—at least one Sunday out of a month.... We went there to Bible School—yeah. A lot of the girls went to the Bible School, so we went along also. But after we got there, we did learn a lot.*

Mary Helen Berry

My mother was strictly religious. We had to go to church, and...well, I had a boyfriend; if he didn't like church, I didn't keep him, because he had to go to church with me.

William Calhoun

Church, church was not a burden. Church, the church was the hub of activity for the Black children especially at Christmas.... Church was always an integral part of the community. We went to things. We had things. If you belonged to Corinthian, you know, they were known for their choirs and that was on Mero Street there. First Baptist has been where it's been ever since I've been born, and so has the Methodist Church. So they were always just [an] integral part.

Choir from First Baptist Church, High and Clinton Streets, at the opening session of the state BTU and Sunday school convention, held at Hume Hall, on the Kentucky State campus. The choir was directed by Josephine Krank (standing, with back to camera). Seated: Alice Simpson, Armour Blackburn, Rev. W. R. Hutchison Jr., and Rev. P. A. Carter. In the choir, first row: Atha Mitchell, Reese Wright, Dorothy "Belle" Brown, Lizzie Brown, Brent Roberts, Pat Roberts, Alma Turner, and P. J. Warren; second row: Patricia Brown, Louise Mitchell, Gladys Hutchison, Alex Oden, Arlander Guthrie, unknown, Walter Creal, Ernest Graves, John W. Adams, unknown, Lucille Harris, Caroline Oden, Lillie G. Blackburn, Annie Stone, and unknown; third row: Elizabeth Brown, unknown, and Viola Kellis.

Contributed by Josephine W. Krank

Kimberly Combs at her baptism, with Rev. O. D. Gill, and Bugsy Hall, 1986. Green Hill Baptist Church used Black's Pond, located on Georgetown Road, for baptizing. By 1995, this area was a subdivision known as Silver Lake.

Contributed by Bernice Combs

The St. John A.M.E. sanctuary, ca. 1990s.

Contributed by Carrie Watts

Henry Kemp

Mason Burton: *What church did your family attend?*

Kemp: *First Baptist. I sang in the choir, I guess I call myself teaching Sunday school. As I've gotten older I've realize I don't know that much about the Bible, but I can put it in my words and make you understand it. I did that kitchen down there, Harold Hogan and I; I did that table up there in the front communion—well, I put it back together …and they still use it. I enjoyed myself and those same kids that I taught, sang in the choir and things like that; I started the quartet…. Max [and] Scott Jameson's daddy [Scott Jameson], and I can't remember the other fellows.*

First Baptist Choir at the Orlando Brown House. The choir sang at the Christmas festivities. Those pictured here include (nearest the wall) Edna Washington, Odessa Green, Catherine Demaree, Mary Helen Berry, Julia Munie, Edmonia Hughley, Maggie Scott, Mary Washington, Karen Moore, and Elizabeth Rodgers.

Contributed by Josephine W. Krank

105

Mary L. McGee

Mason Burton: *I know you were a member of Corinthian Church for a long time, and I remember I was brought up in the Methodist Church, but by the time I reached my teenage years, I just couldn't wait to get to Corinthian. It was, as Flip Wilson says, the church of what's happening now. Tell me about the Corinthian that you…*

McGee: *Oh, the Corinthian I knew was something else. We first started off with a little club. And, Miss Anna Laura Ellis and America Jones was over this little group, and they would also teach us the Bible, and then we would have picnics and then we would get together, not only Corinthians, but all the churches of the youth would get together and a lot of times we'd have hayrides. Now, Dee Samuels would always find this truck and have it all full of hay and all and would take us on these little picnics, and we'd have wiener roasts and marshmallows. And whatever we started out, we started out with prayer, even the picnics and all.*

So after Miss America [Jones] married and she moved, and Mrs. Ellis kept us for a while, and then after she started having her children, she could no longer do it. Well, by that time I was a nice teenager, mostly around, I guess, about sixteen or seventeen, I just had to take over this club, but I wanted to make it into a choir. And that's what I done. So I made a choir out of our little club. We had about thirty, and we would always go up on the campus most of the time. When we first started out, Barbara Collins and Mary played for the choir. Mary Smither and Barbara Smither at that time. So then after Mary left, and as Barbara said, we got too good for her to play, so then, Reverend [Charles] King was the minister at the church at the time, and he and I would go up on the campus every Wednesday night and pick up whoever wanted to play, so we ended up, I guess, with about, I guess we had about fifteen different students that went to Kentucky State that would come down and play for us. And, the last ones that we ended up with was Marion Rogers and Charles Little.

Now, Charles Little was over the youth choir…at that time we were a teenage choir, and then we gave our choir a name which ended up to be the Temple Choir. And I don't know of any place in Kentucky that we didn't sing at the time.…We went to Florida, we sang there, we sang at Harlan, Kentucky.… But at that time at Corinthian, everybody would rush to get dressed to get to church so they could get a seat.

The children's choir at Corinthian Baptist Church, ca. 1958.

Contributed by Evelyn Williams

The locally renowned Temple Choir at Corinthian Baptist Church. Front row: Rev. Charles N. King, Barbara Collins, Emma White, Barbara Fields White, Madge Williams, Donna Fields, Cornelia Fields; second row: Camellia Million, Toni Davis, Christine Washington, Mary Lucy McGee; back row: Charles Little, Jeff McGee, Arthur Kenny Redding, Jeffrey White, Marion Rodgers, Robert "Sarge" Redding, June White.

Contributed by Cornelia F. Calhoun

Mason Burton: *Including me.*

McGee: *So they could get a seat and then when our Reverend got real sick, then we continued to hold the church together through singing. And it was the same way. Everybody rushing to get there to get a seat. And, then we'd have different ministers to come in to preach on that Sunday morning until, you know, we elected another minister to take over. But, it was a good choir and we had a good cooperation, and everybody loved to sing, plus we had a shouting choir.*

Mason Burton: *Amen for that.*

Barbara F. White

Boyd: *Let's talk about Corinthian. Where was Corinthian located?*

White: *It was on Mero Street. And there was an alley right across from Corinthian Street that took you up to the junk yard and on up to Clinton Street. We went to Sunday school. It was a big church. In the front was the sanctuary and on the back there were two stories. The classrooms were on the second floor. They had a kitchen. We would go to church, and then later in years, I joined the choir there.*

Boyd: *Well, this choir wasn't just a normal choir, though. I've heard about this choir.*

White: *And the Temple Choir went everywhere. We went as far as Gary, Indiana, to sing.… We were a good choir.… I'd say there were about twenty, twenty-five people in that choir.… The Temple Choir went on from like sometime in the late sixties, through about in the eighties.*

Boyd: *Do you remember some of the songs?*

White: *"Didn't It Rain." What else? "Blessed Assurance." Plus, we wouldn't sing the traditional arrangements. Marion Rogers was the choir director. He would arrange them another way. And then after Marion left, Dowell Taylor became our director.… Several of us got together to sing at Corinthian's hundred and twenty-fifth anniversary last year. And Marion played for us. He's over on Main Street in Lexington. He came back and played for us.*

William Calhoun

Our teachers went to church; so, they were always a part of us.... They were part of the community. They just didn't teach. They lived it. A good teacher that's worth their salt just doesn't give information. They live the life that they teach the children to become.

Clinton Street High School graduating class, 1914. The photo was taken at Frankfort High School, hence the FHS banner displayed in the background. First row: Ada Garner Carson, Ernestine Hayes, unknown, Apperline Hayes; back row: Katie Hancock Brown, unknown, Marie Garner Robinson, unknown. Photo by H. A. Gretter.

Contributed by Mattie Davis

"BEING SOMEBODY"

•EDUCATION•

"Be quiet boy; you might learn something."

Clarence Johnson,
Mayo-Underwood History Teacher

EDUCATION HAS ALWAYS BEEN IMPORTANT in the Black community. To many it was an essential means of improving one's status within the community and enhancing one's career opportunities. Under segregation, public education for Blacks was often inferior and woefully inadequate. Yet, the presence of the Clinton Street (1884–1928), the Mayo-Underwood (1929–1964), and Rosenwald (1917–1977) schools, along with the unique and invaluable institution of Kentucky State University (originally Kentucky State Normal School for Colored Persons), founded in 1887, meant that Frankfort and Franklin County Blacks enjoyed more educational resources than African Americans in many other Kentucky communities. Thus, late-nineteenth- and early-twentieth-century Frankfort was a leading educational center for African Americans in the state. Years have gone by since Clinton Street and Mayo-Underwood closed and Rosenwald changed status. Yet, the memories of those who attended, taught, or sent their children to these schools are filled with praise and pride for these beloved institutions that provided segregated public instruction for the city and county.

Schools were at the epicenter of community life, serving more than the community's youth. Although primarily academic institutions, the schools regularly hosted meetings that had little to do with academic life and everything to do with vital community issues. Moreover, the schools provided a focal point, a unifying institution, for all Black residents. Rural and urban youth, children from geographically remote areas and from different economic backgrounds, were forced to interact by necessity of circumstances. And as the schools brought the youth throughout the community together, it did likewise with the adults. Parents and community leaders invested time and effort in school-related events, such as graduation ceremonies. Those long lines of kindergarteners in white caps and gowns, eighth graders in white dresses and white suit coats, and seniors in blue caps and gowns were seen as rites of passages recognized by the entire community. Fund-raisers and athletic accomplishments also encouraged broad participation. Thus, the annual Rosenwald Bazaar, sponsored by the PTA to raise money for playground equipment, trips, etc., and the Mayo-Underwood fund-raising carnivals were community-wide efforts, both complete with all kinds of food and treats, games, prizes, and even fortunetellers.

Perhaps one of the strongest remembrances was the schools' ties to the Black churches. In terms of importance to Black life, who can say which came first—the schoolhouse or the church? Centenarian Millie Combs set the stage in her memories with: "We didn't have a schoolhouse...it was a church—one room. You could go on Sundays and all had church and sang. We went back in the schoolhouse and had church." In her mind, as in early practice, the two became one. Teachers often promoted religious education and encouraged youth to participate in revivals and other church-sponsored activities. In turn, the churches encouraged and supported the schools by mobilizing the Black community. Christian principles of morality and behavior also went to school on Monday morning, that is before religion and education went their separate ways. In fact, Black children learned many of the old inspirational songs and hymns, like "Bless This House" and "Little Old Church in the Wildwood," under the fingertips of school music teacher Etta Blanton. Morning devotional rituals were a standard part of the day. Mary Lucy McGee remembers that, "In the morning we would start off that morning with prayer and a song, and then a teacher would always read scripture and she would have us all to learn a quotation." Teachers, parents, and community strictly enforced hard work, sobriety, and punctuality—and accompanying behavior.

Testimonies of those on the receiving end of segregated education are laden with stories about their teachers. Mary Ellis's memory takes us back several decades to the early years of Clinton Street School:

> We had good teachers.... I mean good teachers who wanted to see the children learn and be interested. We had one teacher named Winnie Scott, I always felt she burned the midnight oil. They didn't have electricity yet, lamp light...always interested in making you worthwhile and going out into the world.

(Mrs. Ellis was too modest to claim herself as one of these special teachers—but she was.)

Most of the Black educators were more than just teachers to their students. They served as role models, community leaders, and living examples of the benefits of an education, oftentimes demonstrating a concern and caring for youth that extended well beyond the classroom. Many former students speak of their teachers with respect, love, and admiration. They were remembered in awe, like Ora Mae Cheaney who "took us home with her for continuing after-hours education." They were remembered for their personal talents, like Mary Holmes and her culinary skills for making pull candy or Ruby Dixon's musical abilities. They were remembered as disciplinarians who insisted on respect and appropriate behavior from their students, like Ora J. Caise, who lovingly educated her third-grade classes at Mayo-Underwood with the assistance of her trusted companion, a doubled black telephone wire known as "Willie." These educators, while caring, compassionate, and concerned, could, and often did, enforce high standards of conduct in the classroom. Respect for elders was expected—and demanded. The word from Rosenwald students was that Mazie Boclair would grab a student by the ear and twist it when things couldn't be settled otherwise. Yet, she was dearly loved and nobody worried about "child abuse" then. In the 1999 dedication of the memorial monument to Mayo-Underwood, Van Warren quipped that if Mayo-Underwood's teachers were teaching now, most of them would be sitting in jail.

Obviously, the schools were a major factor in community social life, particularly for youth. Non-academic clubs and activities such as band, drama, and homemakers were vital elements in school social life and provided an opportunity for young Blacks to undertake leadership roles among their peers. The schools encouraged broad extra-curricular activities for their students and were also the anchor for youth-based organizations, such as Helen Holmes's and Edna Patton's Girl Scout troops at Rosenwald, Edmonia Hughley's Girl Scout troop at Mayo-Underwood, and Pauline Manley's 4-H Clubs at both schools.

Both Mayo-Underwood and Rosenwald were instrumental in many Black students' developing and cultivating an appreciation for the arts and humanities. Teachers and the PTA at Rosenwald promoted community involvement with the Louisville Symphony Orchestra's special concerts, to which children and teachers from all city schools were invited. Students passing through Alice Samuel's classes at Mayo-Underwood were encouraged to memorize poetry and taught the fine art of recitation. Both schools had elaborate all-school theatrical productions featuring music and dance presentations at the end of the school year. These programs not only enriched cultural life, they provided an opportunity to showcase local talent. That such exposure would result in leadership development in the arts was no accident. And because of this, Frankfort can boast of a George Wolfe and a Mark Warren in theatre and film and a Brooks Giles and a Leonard Brown in music. While these noted figures generate community pride and inspiration, there are hundreds of others who without recognition or publicity have committed themselves to the cause of education in Frankfort's African American community.

Kentucky State University's impact on the Black community in Frankfort is immeasurable. The university's resources played a vital role in providing expertise and facilities when segregation barred the use of other public meeting places. Kentucky State provided student teachers, teacher training, research and conferencing opportunities, and a labor pool of post-secondary students to assist elementary and secondary educators. Additionally, the university's presence in the community (via faculty participation in local churches and civic groups, community activities held on campus, homecoming festivities, etc.) led numerous youth to transition naturally from high school to enrollment at KSU. There was always somebody trained, or in training, to help with the senior citizens, Girl Scouts, or summer camps and playground activities, to referee a football or basketball game. Sororities, fraternities, local organizations, and churches offered scholarships to local high-school graduates to encourage them to go on to college. And KSU's homecoming activities served as the basis for a community-wide celebration that involved more than just the institution's alumni.

Although integration of Frankfort's elementary- and secondary-school systems affected Black education in both subtle and dramatic, as well as positive and negative, ways, it remains unchanged that education offers the best and most certain means of economic and social advancement to area youth. We must work together to encourage more Black college students to become the modern-day counterparts of Laura Chase, James B. and Ione Brown, W. W. and Susie Jones, Minnie J. Hitch, Asbury Jones, Mildred Jacobs, Marianne Hanley, Anna M. Wolfe, Robert Williams, Pattye Simpson, and so many, many others.

We must also support and sustain the mission of Kentucky State University in furthering this objective. Generations of Black educators have passed a torch to us and we must not let them, or our children, down.

Old Clinton Street School students and faculty. Mrs. Winnie A. Scott is first seated on left.

Contributed by Margurite Shauntee

Josephine Krank

Krank: *I don't remember too much about my childhood, but when I came here at six years old, when I started to school everybody I knew was in the third grade, and so I skipped the second grade and went to the third grade.*

Fletcher: *What school was it?*

Krank: *Clinton Street...I started in the third grade, and then they closed Clinton Street and built Mayo-Underwood. I was a 1932 graduate of Mayo-Underwood.... They built Mayo-Underwood and then closed Clinton 'cause they decided they'd have to bring it up from behind the prison.*

Fletcher: *Where did Black children go for high school before Mayo-Underwood?*

Krank: *Clinton Street. Clinton went through high school.*

Clinton Street High School, elementary class, 1909. First row: Robert Mason, J. Booker Simpson, Flem Holman, James Vaughn Morton, Murray Conda, Carlton Ellis, Claude Higton, J. Adams, James Morton, Sonny Lenn, Charlie Page, Jerry Samuels, Alford Childs; second row: Callie Harvey, Mattie Garner, Claudia Higton, Jacquelin Williams, Cecelia Paey, Katie Winters, Orthello Gaines, Cornelia Warren, Harriett Robinson, Mary E. Tracey, Viola Anderson; third row: Billy Booker, Booker Washington, Clifford Cannada, Minnie Hawkins, Marie Wooldridge, Jonnie Ward, Mary Lucy Parker, Sarah Clay, America Higgins, Margaret Allen, Mattie Wooldridge, Virginia Mayse, Winfred Mitchell, Thomas Gatewood, Henry Hampton; fourth row: Miss Mamie Woolfolk (teacher), Coleman Garner, Churchill Carter, _____ Scrubs, Underwood Taylor, Professor Mayo (principal), Joe Lindsey, Henry Ellis, Bert Paey, Claude Dotson, Earl Higgins, Thomas Graham.

Contributed by Mary E. Ellis

Clinton Street faculty.

Contributed by Margurite Shauntee

Clarence Williams

Now, I don't want to take anything away from Clinton Street, because that was the beginning of all of it. Clinton Street was a good school.

Margaret Ellis

I went one year at Clinton Street [School] in the kindergarten. And they had the school finished down here, and, then, I went in the second grade in the new school. Miss Naomi was my teacher.

Teacher Marjorie Hall, standing at back, and her Clinton Street School class. Among those pictured are Lucille Linn, Matthew Sales, ___ Marshall, Johnny Spenser, Leon Pool, James "Buddy" Ellis, Raymond Carnval, Charles Johnson, Elizabeth Redding, William Buckner, and Wilson Linn.

Contributed by George E. Mitchell

PRINCIPAL, TEACHERS AND CLASS OF 1909 CLINTON STREET HIGH SCHOOL

Postcard of Clinton Street High School class of 1909, shown with their teachers and Professor Mayo (principal, seated at center).

Contributed by Josephine W. Krank

Henry Sanders

I went to Clinton Street [School], the old school up behind the prison [Kentucky State Penitentiary]. See, we went past the prison to go to school every day. I saw the first graduation class at Mayo-Underwood. The principal [who] used to be at Clinton Street High School was named Mayo [Professor William H. Mayo]. And [E. E.] Underwood is the...black doctor in Frankfort.... They decided to name it for the principal of Clinton Street and the doctor, and they came up with Mayo-Underwood.

Exterior of the Mayo-Underwood High School, located at Mero and Wilkinson Streets.

Contributed by Mattie Davis

Glenn Douglas

Mason Burton: *Well, tell me about Mayo-Underwood Elementary School.*

Douglas: *I guess, I was about five years old when I started there. And, it was a lot of discipline there…. I don't remember my first teacher. But I remember Ms. [Ora Jane] Caise, [Laura F.] Chase, Ms. [Mary C.] Holmes, my fifth- and sixth-grade teacher, Ms. Holmes, I think, was my third- and fourth-grade teacher. And Ms. Chase was my eighth-grade teacher. Ms. [Etta] Blanton was the seventh-grade teacher. And I think Ms. Chase was the last teacher I had and she was a disciplinarian. So was Ms. Caise. Ms. Caise would…send us down on the river bank to Sandbar to get our own switches. And she called her switches "Little Willie." And she would say, "I hear you calling me." And she would whip my butt with those switches, you know, 'cause I was, ah, I was a little rascal. I was always getting into something at all times.*

Margaret Ellis

They [local Black teachers] were really…really educated people with all kinds of degrees. One thing about it, they had concern for you. I mean, if they saw you was getting behind [in your studies] they would work with you, you know. They'd stay in school and work with you.

Wesley Marshall Jr.

Mason Burton: *Where did you go to school?*

Marshall: *Mayo-Underwood, it was a grade school and a high school together. We had the*

Mayo-Underwood faculty, 1939–40. The teachers took on different classes as needed. 1) Mary Holmes, 7th grade; 2) Marietta Tucker Paey, 3rd grade; 3) J. B. Brown, principal, also chemistry and physics; 4) Alice D. Samuels, English and typing; 5) Ora Jane Caise, 4th grade; 6) Ora Mae Williams Cheaney, home economics and National Homemakers Association; 7) Mary Elizabeth Lindsay Barker, 1st and 2nd grades; 8) Cornelia Warren Bennett, librarian and 1st and 2nd grades; 9) Etta Banks Blanton, music; 10) Apperline Hayes, 8th grade or English and typing; 11) Marie Robinson, 6th grade or lower; 12) Clarence S. Johnson, math, history, and social science; 13) Dorothy Wilson, 2nd grade and librarian; 14) Laura F. Chase, 8th grade; 15) Asbury Jones, coach and physical education; 16) Murray Conda, manual arts and shop.

Contributed by Josephine Calhoun

football field, you know, we played football, basketball, baseball.

Mason Burton: *Tell me about some of your teachers, the ones you liked the best.*

Marshall: *Well, I liked Ms. Mary C. Holmes and I liked Ms. Dorothy Wilson…[Elizabeth] Lindsey and Ms. Etta Blanton.… They had a nice personality about them. They were strict on you.… The learning was there, but you had to be the one to take it up.*

Mason Burton: *Tell me a little about Miss Holmes, because she played such a prominent role in most of our lives.*

Marshall: *Well, she took me under her wing, her and Ms. Chase. And they gave me little odds and ends jobs, you know, so I wouldn't be out here after scuffling, you know, to make ends meet and things. Ms. Holmes used to buy me clothes. Miss Chase used to buy me clothes. Then they used to take me and I worked for them around the house. Miss Mary C. Holmes, she had a big, big garden down here on the Sandbar, and I used to take care of it for her. So, we raised turnips down in there and I took care, was the overseer of her garden. So, all the kids when they get out of school, they would come down there to the Sandbar and I'd take them down there and get them some turnips. Well, Ms. Holmes come down there, and she said, "Wesley," she said, "my turnips are missing." I told her I let some of the kids down there and I give them some turnips. So, when I go back to school, she had me writing "turnips" five hundred times on…a great big old sheet of paper. And I was writing big, you know, she said, "You're going to have to get another sheet," so, I started writing small.*

Professor Clarence Johnson, history teacher at Clinton Street High and Mayo-Underwood High School, taken in the late 1920s.

Contributed by Josephine W. Krank

Vocalists, the Samuelites, taken at a concert, September 3, 1937. The members were John Wesley Lewis, bass; Ellsworth Marshall Jr., baritone; William G. Leathers Jr., lead second tenor; Thomas McKee, first tenor; and Alice D. Samuels, director.

Contributed by Josephine W. Krank

117

They [Mayo-Underwood Teachers] were dedicated teachers, they were stern. They were people who were interested in you, to know that you had come there to learn...and when you catch on, you make a

Teachers from Mayo-Underwood School attended a teachers' conference on the Kentucky State campus, ca. 1940s. Alice D. Samuels, unknown, Mary Holmes, Elizabeth Lindsey, Ora Mae Cheaney, Dorothy Wilson, Laura Franklin, Laura Chase, Ora Caise.

Contributed by Cornelia F. Calhoun

Sallie Fields with Mayo-Underwood teachers Mary Holmes, Dorothy Wilson, and Edmonia Hughley at Natural Bridge State Park.

Contributed by Cornelia F. Calhoun

M. L. Mastin and Robert Williams, instructors at Mayo-Underwood School, ca. 1950s.

Contributed by Billie Mack Johnson

118

good student. Patience is what they had. And you had to get your work or you just wouldn't make it. So, being as they were and making us as they hoped we would be, made good students.

Mary McGee

Mason Burton: *Where did you go to school?*

McGee: *Mayo-Underwood High. We started in elementary all the way through.*

Mason Burton: *You have any fond memories?*

McGee: *Oh, Lord, yes, I loved Mayo-Underwood. We—'course we'd have times to play, and we would play jacks or run, and hide and go seek, all the kids' games then.*

Mason Burton: *When you were in the elementary school, what was a typical day like? I mean, you would go to school, I guess at eight in the morning…*

McGee: *In the morning, we would start off that morning with prayer and a song, and then a teacher would always read scripture, and she would have us all to learn a quotation. And, every morning, we had to say a quotation, and she wouldn't let nobody say, "Jesus wept." Everybody had to learn a different quotation besides "Jesus wept." That was, let me see, Miss Caise and Miss Chase. And, then we had Mrs. Paey. She was the third-grade teacher at that time. And she belonged to the same church I did at that time, and she would also have us do the same thing in her class—start off with prayer, and we'd sing a song, "America the Beautiful," or something like that…. And then we'd start off with our classes. And, we didn't change classes. We just stayed in one class and that one teacher at that time taught everything.*

Clara E. Hogan

Fletcher: *What are the kinds of things you remember about Mayo-Underwood?*

Hogan: *Well, I graduated from Mayo-Underwood in '46…. I have a lot of fond memories of Mayo-Underwood…. Very good school relationships; didn't have to bother about race and violence and drugs, but getting along with the teachers—just one big happy family…. Professor James Brown was the principal when I went there. Mrs. Etta Blanton was a teacher; Alice Samuels was our English teacher…. Mrs. Cheaney was our Home Economics teacher—we loved Mrs. Cheaney.*

Margaret Ellis

He [Professor James Brown] was our freshman teacher [at Mayo-Underwood], and we used to tell him all the time…because he…was really educated. And we didn't know what he was talking about half the time. And we said, "You've got too much education to be teaching us. Shoot, we don't know what you're saying."

Henrietta Gill

There were things they didn't get paid for…. Once I wanted to take typing and Ms. Apperline Hays was our teacher. The typing class was full because I didn't make up my mind till the last minute that I wanted to take it. She would bring her portable typewriter to school every day and teach me typing. And she lived in South Frankfort now. She walked over there…and she brought a little portable typewriter with her to teach me to type. I mean, this is the kind of teachers we had. Yes. They were dedicated.

Mayo-Underwood students at corner of Mero and Center Streets, looking west. David Gaines, Charles Richard Payne, Lewis Payne, Robert Hogan, Samuel Clowney, and Richard Williams.

Contributed by Edna Rawlings Washington

Mayo-Underwood students seated on the steps of the Mero and Center Streets corner of the school, ca. 1955–56. Lolita Harvey, Katherine Demaree, Jeanette Williams, Maxine Brown, Barbara Fields, Georgetta Evans.

Contributed by Katie Johnson Graham

Group relaxing on Washington Street after a school day at Mayo-Underwood High School, ca. 1950s. Mary Jones Washington, Anna Berry Combs, Lauretta Clay, Marsha Williams, Roberta Jennels, Jeanette Williams, Maggie Combs, Lewverna Jacobs, and Frank Hall.

Contributed by Harry Craig

Barbara White

Boyd: *What I hear about Mayo-Underwood is that it was the most wonderful school...*

White: *Well, I enjoyed going there. And I started there in the first grade and went all the way. And I was the last graduating class, high school class.... The teachers were interesting. They took pride in the students. And we had to do our homework, they made sure of that. And if you didn't do right, well, we had a source right there in the school to tell, so we always did right. Because if they'd tell Daddy Henry anything, then he'd tell Mama and then we had it. But none of my brothers or sisters, they weren't rowdy people. They were studious, you know, go to school, do what you have to do, and learn. In fact, I ended up being the valedictorian of my graduating class.*

John Sykes

We had a little lunchroom down there and had a lot of those powdered eggs and war surplus that they cooked. Peanut butter. I remember that peanut butter. They'd give us big cans of it. And we'd have...peanut butter crackers and chocolate milk for the break. And then they would have a wholesome meal at lunch. I think it cost about...seventy-five cents a week.

Mary Helen Berry

My brother, he was one of the original [founding members] of the Grad Club. They had that first meeting at his [Mark Warren's] house on a Sunday.... They were interested in Colored children, and they wanted to keep the athletics going and to help the parents that couldn't afford to help their children.

Mayo-Underwood High School football team in the early 1940s. Kneeling: Lonnie Gurton. First row: William I. Fields, Bernard "Buster" Shannon, ____Childs, ____Basey, George Tall; second row: Fletcher Davis, ____Caldwell, Calvin Payne, Bill Hume, Kenneth Childs, Dorsey Brown, George Calhoun.

Contributed by Josephine Calhoun

Twelve-year-old William "Willie" Washington shooting basketball on the Mayo-Underwood Sandbar, ca. 1949. The Sandbar was the playground for all Mayo-Underwood students and was also used for physical education classes. It was located across the street from the high school and flooded often.

Contributed by William G. Washington

Henry Sanders

The Grad Club was supposed to have been for graduates of Mayo-Underwood High School…to help the old athletic department because they never could get enough money to fund the athletic department. Buying equipment…balls and uniforms…. They'd give a dance every commencement for the graduates and have Smoke Richardson's dance band…. They was out of Lexington. We help the local high students who are aspiring to go to college. We got a scholarship fund set up. Jack Robb started it in '33 or in '34…right after he got out of high school.

Henry and Margaret Ellis

Margaret Ellis: *We had socials [at school]….We didn't call them dances. We had socials and Ms. Holmes would chaperone.*

Henry Ellis: *After the basketball game, we would have a social. All right, at ten o'clock you still had to [go] home. Your mama was out there waiting on you, and your dad was out there waiting on you.*

Margaret Ellis: *Oh, they was looking at you dancing.*

Barbara White

Yeah. There were activities. They'd have a few dances. But we were so into the classroom stuff that by the time we got home in the afternoons, you know, we were too tired to do anything else. But they had baseball and a basketball team while I was in school. I don't remember them having football when I was in school, because I think they had discontinued that, but they did have basketball. We were involved in the New Homemakers of America, NHA, which was in our Home Ec class. And we would have meetings, and we ended up going to like the state conference, which was at Kentucky State, which was very

William Washington, taking a shot at the goal on the night he scored 50 points for the Mayo-Underwood Tigers against Georgetown High, ca. 1955. The team was coached by Alvin Hanley.

Contributed by William G. Washington

exciting for us. Maxine Brown, who was one of my classmates, and I went to Daytona Beach, Florida, in our junior year, all by ourselves. My mother took us to Louisville and put us on the train, the South Wind, and we went to Daytona Beach to the national conference. It was real exciting.

The Mayo-Underwood High basketball team before a game at the school, 1955. Front row: Tom Robb, William "Dicky" Dixon, Robert Marshall; back row: Robert Demaree, Frederick Green, Cassius Ellis, Clarence Marshall, William Washington, Charles Blythe. William Washington was the most outstanding player of Frankfort. He went on to play for KSU. He played basketball abroad and later coached both girls' and boys' basketball for 28 years.

Contributed by William G. Washington

New Homemakers of America (NHA) at the Mayo-Underwood School, ca. 1955–56. Ora Mae Cheaney served as their advisor and home economics teacher. Left to right: Barbara Fields, president; Mary Washington, vice president; Jeanette Williams, secretary; Lolita Harvey, assistant secretary; Cornelia Fields, treasurer; Dorothy Combs, reporter; Katie Graham, historian; Maxine Brown, song leader; Geneva Combs, parliamentarian.

Contributed by Cornelia F. Calhoun

Donald Hudspeth, Dorothy Combs McGowan, Harry Craig, Geneva Combs Craig, Maggie Combs, and William Stallard prepare for the 1956 prom at Mayo-Underwood High School.

Contributed by Harry Craig

Prom at Mayo-Underwood High School, 1956. Maggie Combs, Mary Jones Washington, Geneva Combs Craig, Dorothy Combs McGowan (prom queen), Jeanette Williams Chatmon, Hattie Belle Boyd, Elizabeth Rodgers Rudolph.

Contributed by Harry Craig

Graduating Class

Howard Allen
James E. Brown
Charles R. Childs
Clara B. Childs
Mary Lucy Chinley
Robert Lee Ellis
James T. Graham
Paul V. Graham
Anthony A. Haynes II

William W. Jones II
Thomas L. Johnson
William F. Martin
Jennie E. Mitchell
Barbara D. Metcalf
Mary R. Poole
Alex Sanders
Bridgget J. Smither
Clarence A. Williams

Lucille N. Williams

William W. Jones II .... Highest Ranking
William F. Martin .... Second Ranking

HOME ECONOMICS

Mary B. Brown
Annie E. Combs
Mary J. Davis
Ecla E. Hunter

Emily T. Saunders
Mary H. Sears
Mary P. Smither
Dorothy E. Washington

Evelyn J. Williams

Commencement Exercises

Mayo-Underwood High School
Frankfort, Kentucky

June 1–6, 1947

Baccalaureate Services

Auditorium

JUNE 1, 1947   4 P. M.

Processional

"Fairest Lord Jesus"—Crusader's Hymn .... Chorus

Invocation

"Holy City"—Stephen Adams .... William Moole

Baccalaureate Sermon .... Rev. Garland K. Offutt
Dean Simmons University, Louisville, Ky.

"A Mighty Fortress"—Martin Luther .... Chorus

Benediction

Recessional

(Audience will please remain seated during Recessional)

Class Night, June 2, 8:15 P. M.

Awards Day Assembly, June 5, 10:30 A. M.

Graduation Exercises

Auditorium

JUNE 4, 1947   8:15 P. M.

William F. Martin, Presiding

Processional

"Lead Me Lord"—Samuel Wesley .... Chorus

Invocation .... Rev. W. A. Smither

"I Heard A Forest Praying"—Peter De Rose .... Chorus

Graduation Address .... Rev. J. Aston Hill
Louisville, Kentucky

"Road to Mandalay"—Alex Speaks .... Thomas Johnson

Awarding of Certificates and Diplomas .... Supt. C. D. Redding

Presentation of Awards .... Prin. J. E. Brown

"Gloria Murra!" .... Ensemble

Benediction

Recessional

(Audience will please remain seated during Recessional)

Mayo-Underwood High School 1947 commencement program.

Contributed by Thomas Johnson

John Sykes

They complained about the books, but they were the same books they had at Second Street and at Frankfort High. I think we had better teachers, because they didn't teach you what was in the book, they taught you what life was about.... When those guys talked, they were history. They knew from the time when people were slaves, almost. Their grandparents and their parents were slaves. And they told us about how things had changed.... They taught us about life and a lot of things. They taught us about food and hygiene.... They wouldn't dare teach that at Frankfort High. But they wanted you to be clean, solid, healthy citizens later on, so they took that extra step. Plus, they knew everybody's grandmama.

But the teachers were real stern back then.... Miss Caise and Miss Holmes and some of the teachers, especially elementary school. They would have competition in class. And they would give out candy and they'd let you sit in a row based on your grades for the week. And some of these guys,...it just gave them some kind of competition and it made some of them get involved that wouldn't, especially for the candy, now. Because they made great candy. Miss Holmes's pulled candy and Miss Caise's chocolate candy, we'd hustle for that.

Barbara White

Boyd: *What year did you graduate?*

White: *Nineteen fifty-seven. There was seven people in our class...one boy.*

Boyd: *How many of those seven did you feel like went all the way through with you?*

White: *Yes. Roberta Jennels, Maggie Combs went to Rosenwald. Geneva went to Rosenwald. Raymond [Harris] went to Rosenwald. Lolita Harvey, she went all the way through. I went all the way through. Who else was in that class? Two of the people in that class now are deceased. But we, all of us, out of the seven, three, four of us went all the way through, from first grade, because they didn't have kindergarten when I was going to school. They started, I think, the year after I started school.*

Mayo-Underwood class of 1948. Emily Sanders, Anna E. Combs, Reba Hunter, Dorothy Washington, Mary Smither, Joe Spencer, Mary Helen Campbell, Evelyn Williams, Mary Belle Brown, Al Williams, Mary Julia Davis.

Contributed by Evelyn Williams

John Sykes

Sykes: *We went to high school, Frankfort High School, I think in fifty-seven.*

Boyd: *'57?*

Sykes: *Yeah, that was the year they integrated. Actually, they integrated the year before that, because we lost our shop teacher and we couldn't get one replaced in such a short time. We had a hard time getting teachers anyway. A lot of them were doubling up, like the math teacher to teach science and sometime he'd be teaching shop.... 1956 we lost our shop teacher, so that's when integration actually started. We went to class over to Frankfort High over to their shop and walked back over to Mayo-Underwood after that one. So we could go there to shop. Just for that one class.*

So the next year, I think that's probably when they passed those laws. And they said, you've got a choice, you can go to Frankfort High or Mayo-Underwood. Well, a lot of us wanted to play football, and we'd didn't have a football team over to Mayo-Underwood. I think Dunbar out of Lexington put a finish to our football team. They put most of them in the hospital, and we didn't have a team anymore after that. And we wanted to play football, so we went to Frankfort High.

Margaret Berry

They took the school away from us. If they'd let us alone, left our teachers alone, the school would have been there and our children would have learned something. Now, they go to school. These people don't care nothing about them. They don't push them.... We got some come out of Mayo-Underwood as lawyers and doctors and everything.

Catherine and Johnny Demaree pose after his graduation ceremony from Frankfort High, ca. 1961.

Contributed by Josephine W. Krank

Frankfort native Brooks Giles III as drum major for Franklin County High School, ca. 1981–82. Giles has gained an international reputation as a tenor saxophonist and leader of the Brooks Giles Quartet based in New York City. Touring Europe and Asia, he has performed before presidents and royalty.

Contributed by Gloria Giles

127

Mason Burton: *You're here this weekend for the Mayo-Underwood reunion. Apparently, you have some memories from your days there.*

Campbell: *Quite a few memories…I think it was a beautiful school. I liked all the teachers, Professor [James] Brown, Professor [Clarence] Johnson, Professor [Etta] Blanton…quite a few friends and relations, most of them passed on now, I don't think but a few left in my class….*

I graduated in 1933.

Dancing at the Mayo-Underwood 1983 reunion, held at the Capital Plaza Hotel.

Contributed by Josephine W. Krank

Roberta and Clarence Jones, with James B. Johnson (right), at the Mayo-Underwood and Clinton Street School reunion, held at the Frankfort Water Plant Board clubhouse, 1992.

Contributed by Roberta Jennels Jones

Maggie Childs Scott and Clara Elizabeth Hogan at the Mayo-Underwood School reunion picnic, held at the Frankfort Water Plant Board clubhouse, 1994.

Contributed by Clarence Saunders

Workshop for teachers at Kentucky State College, 1946. Many Mayo-Underwood teachers attended.

Contributed by Margurite Shauntee

William Calhoun

My first elementary experience was at Rosenwald.... Rosenwald was a laboratory, so we were always under the microscope to see how we were going to develop. I was there for my first couple of years. Then I was at Mayo-Underwood during the second grade.... I really didn't want to go to Mayo-Underwood, but when you went to Rosenwald, you had a little something to pay. I always loved Rosenwald 'cause I was down there in the old school building and I remember moving to the new school building. Oh, we were proud of our new school. That's why I didn't want to go to Mayo-Underwood....

I graduated in 1963 from Rosenwald Laboratory School.... At that time Anna Mae Wolfe, Dr. Anna Mae Wolfe was teaching. Mrs. [Ruby] Dixon was the music teacher still. Mrs. [Daisy] Evans was still cooking the best macaroni and cheese and apple crisp. When they had fried chicken, honey, she would steam it and put it down in there, oh, lord, we ate back then. That's when you had that old government cheese and butter to make stuff. Oh, man, these people knew how to cook. So when I got back to Rosenwald, it was my delight. And Mildred Jacobs was the younger teacher, you know, for the younger ages.

They used to have what they called student teachers from the college that would come. And I remember

The old three-room Rosenwald School, ca. 1952, locally known as the "Model School." The school was a teacher-training school for elementary education majors at Kentucky State. First row: Kenneth Shauntee, James "Crick" Johnson, Clifton Jones, John Russell Stallard, James Franklin Brown, Freddie Joe Johnson, Martha Ann Patton, Carrie Jacobs, Danny Davis, Robert Harold Dixon, Reginald O'Rourke, Mildretta Jacobs, Nat Edwards, Robert Davis, Emma Laurene Monie; second row: William Stallard, Lewverna Jacobs, Lewis Graham, Henry Exum, next two unknown, Billy Walker, unknown, Ida Marie Brown, Dorothy Combs, Tommy Carter Jr., Bea James, Laura Clay, Sandra Carita Wright, Kenney James; third row: Betty Lou Davis, Carrie James, unknown, unknown, Ronald Guy, Clarence Stallard, unknown, Phyllis Harris, unknown, Donald Hudspeth, unknown, James Davis, George White; fourth row: Joe James, John Henry Guy, Shirley Gaines, unknown, Beverly Overton, Eula Green, unknown, unknown, Jimmy Madison, Dorothy Harris, Virginia Samuels, Mary Catherine Scott; at the top: Doris Jean Evans.

Contributed by Ruby F. Dixon

Class at Rosenwald School, ca. 1957.

Contributed by Winona L. Fletcher

a woman by the name of a Ms. [Mary] Logan and a Ms. Hightower, Brenda Hightower. Oh, I had crushes on those teachers.... Rosenwald was a unique school because they took us to concerts by the Louisville Symphony. So, we had exposure.

Mazie Boclair was our teacher. Mrs. Boclair dealt a lot in ceramics and stuff like that, always making things. But she was an excellent teacher. They dealt very much on things like hygiene and manners. So that you just didn't read, learn how to read and write and do numbers but that you learned how to live, how to bow, how to greet, how to speak. You learned, and if you acted up, she would grab you by your ear and pull it real hard and twist it.... But they were very patient people.

Clarence Williams

Rosenwald, being the laboratory school of Kentucky State University, they were real good. And the kids up there, when they finished the seventh grade, they came to Mayo-Underwood for the eighth grade. And they were wizards.

Clara E. Hogan

Hogan: *We would walk back home up the Hill.... Children who lived on the Hill...they all went to Rosenwald through the eighth grade 'cause that was the county school. See this was the county at that particular time. I think the city limits stopped where the entrance is to Kentucky State now. Kentucky State wasn't in the city; it was in the county—Franklin County.*

Fletcher: *So, the Rosenwald that we know was not there. It was a little brick building.*

Hogan: *I don't know how many yards from where the new building is now, but it was in the same area.... The tunnel wasn't there.... When I first started going to Rosenwald School, the school bus was a bus driven by a horse. 'Course I didn't have to use it 'cause all I had to do was run across the street, and traffic wasn't real heavy then.*

Kindergarten, first-, and second-grade classes of Mazie Boclair Crowley at the "new" Rosenwald Elementary School, ca. 1957. Table at left: Betty Davis and unknown; next table: Charles Solomon or Joe Gilliam; at easel: Don Marshall Jr.; back tables, clockwise beginning with girl seated on end facing camera: Pamela Collins, Dorothy Stallard, Zerlene Lewis, John L. Grevious, Clara Greene, Betty Fletcher, Robert Solomon; at counter in back: Shirley Rodgers; tables at right, Willetta Knight (or Beverly Guy), Pamela Hogan, Anna Thomas (back to camera), Charles Robinson (back to camera).

Contributed by Mattie Davis

George Simmons and Abe Haliburton (with his dog) at "the old slave house" on Kentucky State's farm, ca. 1960s. Simmons lived in the house during his time at Kentucky State. When the house was demolished in 1964, he salvaged a mantel and installed it in his home at College Park.

Contributed by George Simmons

Mary Elizabeth Simmons pretends to milk a cow at Kentucky State's farm, ca. 1940.

Contributed by George Simmons

Margurite Shauntee

The Bazaar was to raise money for the PTA; that was the only thing we did to raise money for the PTA. Now the PTA, at the old school, the PTA built our toilet facility. And then across the street the state had bought the Reed's home—a black family that lived near there—and the PTA people would cook at home and bring it there, and the kids would cross the street for their lunches; they were instrumental in starting the lunch program at Rosenwald....

We had the fishing pond and one of the main things, we had a fortuneteller and she was a former [Fannie] Reid and she married Mr. Roberts that worked on the farm. Of course, she lived in the community and, of course, she would have all the little kids talking to her and telling her who went with who and whatnot and what they were doing—and she would always be the fortuneteller, and she put on all her big beads and rings and things and she would just amaze them; they would just run to you to get money to go to the fortuneteller....

Last school picture of Rosenwald Laboratory School, Kentucky State, 1977. Front row: Stephanie Brooks, Sammy Leonard, Angela Bullie, Paulette Edwards, Kimberly Jacobs, Tonya Davis, Mary Woodard, Wendell Lackey, Jowanna Chris Marshall, unknown, Lonzo Bullie, Shawn Bishop, CaSandra Redding, unknown, Carmen Calhoun, Montobi Mapp, Theodric Allen, Ariana Lackey; second row: Michael Morgan, Brian Pippin, Loren Verhey, Lisa Mayes, Mark Brooks, Tammy Simmons, Lyris Cunningham, Tracy Woodard, Eddie Davis, Cathy Thurman, Michael Douthitt, Stanley Watts, Kymberly Hall, Lisa Oliver, Yvette Jackson, Charles Brooks, Cherie Benson, John Washington, Joann Washington; third row: unknown, Mildred Jacobs, Dionne Parrish, Sara Moore, Leonard Green, Verita Griffen, Alvin Seales, unknown, Melinda Watts, Troy Redd, Glenn Jackson, unknown, Bridget Thurman, Dorisene White, unknown, Ray Simmons, unknown, Leta Epperson, unknown, Deneen White, Pamela McKinney, Mrs. Montgomery, Kirk Brown, Stella Mapp, Mrs. Henry; fourth row: Ralph Bishop, Johnny Mapp, Carlos Wooten, Stevie Wolfe, Phyllis Tillman, Vicki Jones, Susan Oliver, Willie "Bubba" Oliver, Norman Tate, Eric Barnett, Darla White, Nita Robinson, Tim Butler, Bernard Green, Tammy Washington, Carolyn Campbell, Robby Hughley, Gary Payne, Edmond Edwards.

Contributed by Cornelia F. Calhoun

Brothers James and Lindsay Basey boxing on Clinton Street. James won the Golden Gloves Championship in 1939 and 1941.

Contributed by Robert Basey

Henry Kemp

Mason Burton: *We were talking about the students at Mayo-Underwood.*

Kemp: *The boys and girls were some of the best people—they really had the future in mind.... Many of them went to Kentucky State, in fact, the basketball team which I coached at one time, four of them started... for Kentucky State and they won.... One of my favorite students at Mayo-Underwood was Harold Hogan. He reminded me of myself...and I recommended that he go to Kentucky State.... I was hired at Kentucky State so I went there to work and Hogan came to Kentucky State.... Someone asked Professor [James] Brown, who was the [assistant] basketball coach, "What do you think about Harold Hogan as a basketball player?" He said, "I don't know, but when Coach [Joseph] Fletcher calls for his line-up he always calls Hogan's name."*

Kentucky State varsity basketball squad, 1947–48. The team finished the season as runners-up for the M.W.A.A. conference championship. Front row: H. Robinson, L. Hunt, R. Drake, G. Weston, E. Johnson, L. Cavil; second row: Coach Joseph Fletcher, M. Murray, J. Knight, M. Covington, C. Jackson, Assistant Coach C. B. Lewis; back row: H. Wilson, L. Dixon, W. Blair, M. Woolfolk (manager and trainer), R. Roberts, and M. Perkins.

Contributed by Winona L. Fletcher

134

Scott Jameson and James Goss, co-captains of the Kentucky State Thorobreds in 1955–56.

Contributed by Winona L. Fletcher

Max Jameson (number 23) makes a shot for the Kentucky State Thorobreds in the 1950s. The Jameson twins, Scott and Max, both played for Kentucky State. Max later played for the Harlem Globetrotters.

Contributed by Winona L. Fletcher

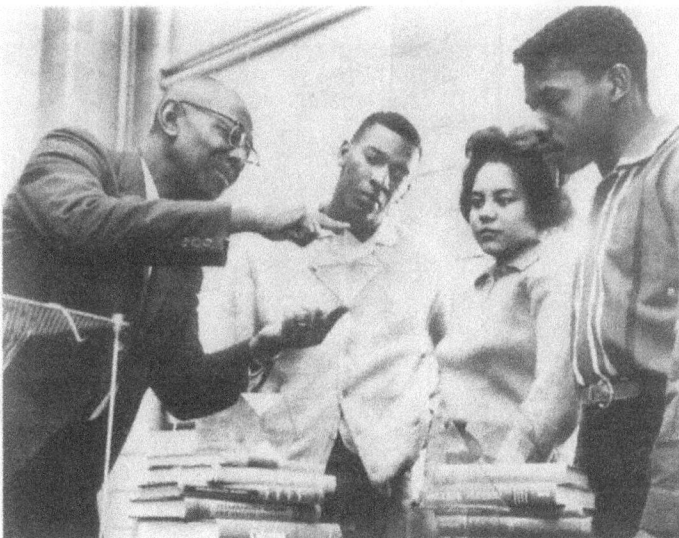

Prof. W. W. Jones, head of the physics and math department, instructs William Leach, Donna Hughes, and another student at Kentucky State, 1965.

Contributed by Winona L. Fletcher

Kentucky State homecoming parade.

Contributed by George Simmons

Archie and Anna Surratt pose in front of Charlotte Wilson's "'40s Oldsmobile" on the Kentucky State campus, ca. 1951. McCullin Hall is in the background.

Contributed by Archie L. Surratt

Gov. Bert Combs meets Kentucky State journalism students from the *Thorobred* staff at the capitol in 1963. Left to right: Gov. Combs, Annjo Twines (Miss Kentucky State, 1963), Viola Amos, and Rochelle Ray.

Contributed by Winona L. Fletcher

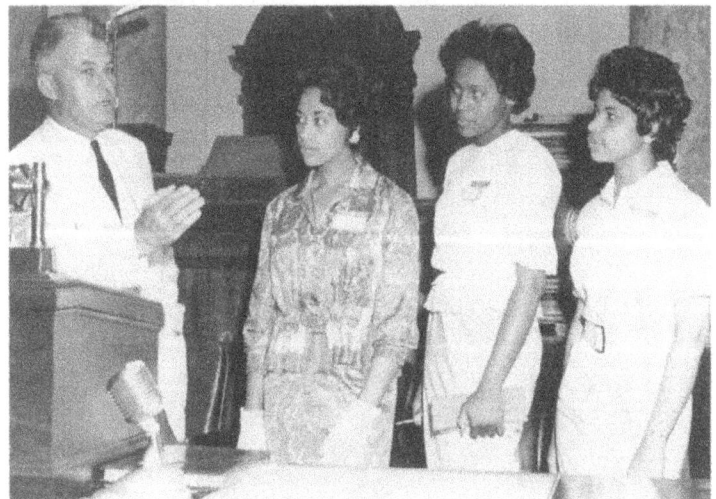

Martin Luther King Jr., speaker at Kentucky State commencement, with President Rufus Atwood, 1957.

Contributed by Helen C. Exum

Helen Holmes

Mother and Dad came to visit me awhile here [Frankfort]. They stayed over for commencement [Kentucky State]. It was a joy for them to see me march in with the faculty and lead our graduating class in. Well, you would have thought I was graduating with a faculty degree myself. Dr. [Rufus] Atwood was the president at that time....

I was the head of the [English] department when I came [to Kentucky State]. They [the students] accused me of being kind of rough. But they also learned. I told them they should learn English, not because they were going to teach it, but they should learn it to guide them through life. I said, to defend yourself.... In other words, it's one of the personal attributes of a successful person to handle language. I still think it is....

Nobody except Dr. Atwood had the love of the old [Kentucky State] graduates. He remembered every person that had been here. He remembered their names. He could call your name. And you see, that to a student after they'd been out a long time means a whole lot.

He was a fine man. When you didn't have an adequate [university] budget, he used to ask... some of us to please come down during [the legislature]. He'd have to plead for his budget, see. So I'd go down and sit in the balcony.

Rehearsing a play at the senior citizens center in the 1970s. Dr. Winona L. Fletcher, Kentucky State drama professor (at center), directs Laverne Eastman and James Scott (seated).

Contributed by Winona L. Fletcher

137

Millie Combs

Combs: *I put them all through high school.*

Mason Burton: *How many children did you have?*

Combs: *Nine.*

Mason Burton: *Nine children?*

Combs: *Two of them went to college. They got scholarships. I couldn't afford, but two of them got scholarships.... They went to Kentucky State.... They went to Rosenwald, that little school, when they were small.... And then they went from there to Mayo-Underwood to high school until Mayo-Underwood closed up. I had one child who hadn't finished Mayo-Underwood. That was Dorothy and she had to go to Elkhorn. She finished at Elkhorn High.*

William Calhoun

Integration helped. Integration also hurt us. When we were segregated, we demanded a lot more. Our teachers were harder on us during the days of segregation than they are today. White teachers didn't demand of us anything because they thought we were dumb as hell anyhow.

Three generations of Kentucky State graduates from one Frankfort family reflect the changing name of the institution. Betty M. Davis, 1973 graduate of Kentucky State University; Mattie Garner Davis, 1960 graduate of Kentucky State College; and Ada Garner Carson, 1932 graduate of Kentucky State Industrial College. Prior to the 1930s, the school was known as the Kentucky Normal and Industrial Institute (KNII).

Contributed by Mattie Davis

CHRONOLOGY

Significant Events in the Black Community
of Frankfort, Kentucky

1775   Daniel Boone leads a group of settlers, including a number of Black laborers, into Kentucky. Susannah Boone Hays and an enslaved Black woman become the first women at Fort Boonesborough.

1777   African Americans comprise about 10 percent of the population at Harrod's Fort.

1778   Settlers at Fort Harrod include 19 Blacks.

Pompey, an African American living with the Shawnee chief Blackfish, plays a central role in the siege of Boonesborough, fighting with the Indians. African American slaves help in the defense of the fort.

1790   The first U.S. Census reports 73,077 persons living in Kentucky, 16 percent of them African American slaves. Free Blacks make up .2 percent of the population.

1792   Kentucky becomes a state, adopting a constitution that legalizes slavery and prohibits the legislature from abolishing slavery without obtaining the consent of the slave owners and compensating them for their property loss.

1800   African Americans in Kentucky number 41,084, almost 19 percent of the population. Free Blacks number 741— or 1.8 percent of the Black population.

1808   The U.S. Congress outlaws the importation of slaves from Africa.

The Kentucky Abolition Society is formed.

1810	African Americans in Kentucky number 82,274, just over 20 percent of the population. Free Blacks number 1,713 — or 2.08 percent of the Black population.
	402 (27%) of Frankfort's 1,099 residents are listed as slaves.
1818	The Kentucky General Assembly passes a law barring free Blacks in other states from migrating to Kentucky.
1820	African Americans in Kentucky number 129,491, almost 19 percent of the population. Free Blacks number 2,759 — or 2.13 percent of the Black population.
	Private day school for Black children opens in Frankfort.
1830	African Americans in Kentucky number 170,130, almost 25 percent of the population. Free Blacks number 4,917 — or 2.9 percent of the Black population.
	Most free Blacks live in segregated enclaves with a strong sense of community.
1833	Whites and Blacks worshipped together until this year; movement to worship separately begins. Black Baptists worship in private homes in Frankfort until the first autonomous congregation builds a church on Clinton Street.
1839	St. John African Methodist Episcopal (A.M.E.) Church is established on Lewis Street. The building and grounds were a gift of Mrs. Triplett to her servants Benjamin Dunmore and Benjamin Hunley.
1840	African Americans in Kentucky number 189,575, just over 24 percent of the population. Free Blacks number 7,317 — or 3.85 percent of the Black population.
	2,846 (30 percent) of Franklin County's 9,420 residents are slaves.
1844	Deed to lot where present church stands made out to First Baptist Church—Clinton Street.
1849	The general assembly repeals the Nonimportation Act, making it legal to bring slaves into Kentucky for resale, and the constitutional convention rejects attempts to abolish slavery.
1859	African Americans in Kentucky number 220,992, about 22.5 percent of the population. Free Blacks number 10,011— or 4.53 percent of the Black population.
	W. H. Gibson Sr. establishes "grammar" (elementary) schools for Blacks in Frankfort.

| 1860 | African Americans in Kentucky number 236,167, almost 20.5 percent of the population. Free Blacks number 10,684 — or 4.52 percent of the Black population. |

1860   African Americans in Kentucky number 236,167, almost 20.5 percent of the population. Free Blacks number 10,684 — or 4.52 percent of the Black population.

1865   The Civil War ends, followed by years of bloodshed, racial violence, Ku Klux Klan activity, and riots in both Frankfort and Franklin County.

1865–80   Several Black areas develop in the city. One of these is "Crawfish Bottom" that was also called "the Craw" or the "Bottom." South Frankfort expands with Second and Third Streets becoming "Black enclaves."

1870   African Americans compose 17 percent of Kentucky's population.

     U.S. Census report for Frankfort: 2,335 Blacks (43 percent) and 3,061 (57 percent) whites. Kentucky's Black Republican leaders meet in Frankfort.

1871   Local Black Democrat Party forms. Also, Mattie Anderson, a white, northern reformer, organizes Frankfort Female High School for Blacks (private).

1870s–80   Efforts by whites to create a segregated society generates increased discrimination, harassment, and violence toward Blacks.

1880   African Americans compose 16 percent of Kentucky's population.

     U.S. Census for Frankfort: 3,199 Blacks (45 percent) and 3,759 (55 percent) whites.

1882   Clinton Street School is constructed, the first facility built specifically for Black education. The principal is nineteen-year-old William H. Mayo.

1886   Kentucky General Assembly passes act to establish a State Normal School for Colored Persons. Seven cities compete for the site; Frankfort is selected when the city council donates a site and $1,500 to locate it in the city.

1887   Jackson Hall is constructed on the site and remains today as Kentucky State University's oldest structure. John H. Jackson, a Black graduate of Berea College, is selected as the first president.

1890   African Americans compose 14 percent of Kentucky's population.

     U.S. Census for Frankfort: 2,634 Blacks (33 percent) and 5,256 (67 percent) whites.

1891   Dr. Edward E. Underwood, a Black physician from Ohio, establishes his medical practice. He becomes an important community leader.

1892   Kentucky General Assembly enacts Separate Coach Law on March 15, 1892, requiring racially segregated public transportation until its formal repeal by the legislature in 1966.

1893   The Independent Colored Baptist Church congregation adopts the name Corinthian Baptist Church. St. John A.M.E. Church congregation builds new edifice on Clinton Street.

1900   African Americans compose 13 percent of Kentucky's population.

U.S. Census for Frankfort: 3,316 Blacks (25 percent) and 9,487 (75 percent) whites. Clinton Street School has eleven faculty and approximately 500 pupils in grades kindergarten through high school.

1902   State Normal School expands curriculum and changes name to Kentucky Normal and Industrial Institute for Colored Persons.

1903   Women's Improvement Club Hospital opens to provide medical care for Franklin County's Black population. Located at 228 East Second Street, it was later renamed Winnie A. Scott Hospital in honor of a local Black teacher whose home was converted into the hospital.

1904   The Kentucky General Assembly passes the Day Law segregating public and private schools, forcing Berea College to end integrated education.

1908   "Practice School" for teacher-education students is established at Kentucky State.

1910   African Americans compose 11 percent of Kentucky's population.

U.S. Census for Frankfort: 2,851 Blacks (27 percent) and 7,614 (73 percent) whites.

The National Association for the Advancement of Colored People (NAACP) is founded.

1918   Blacks from Franklin County in World War I: 113 soldiers and 45 sailors.

1919   Dr. E. E. Underwood establishes NAACP branch in Frankfort.

1920   African Americans compose 9.5 percent of Kentucky's population.

U.S. Census for Frankfort: 2,246 Blacks (22 percent) and 7,558 (78 percent) whites. With leadership from Governor Edwin P. Morrow, the Kentucky General Assembly passes anti-lynching law without a dissenting vote.

1921   Grant from Julius Rosenwald and a sizable donation from citizens leads to construction of a brick "practice school" at Kentucky State.

1926   Kentucky Normal and Industrial Institute changes its name to Kentucky State Industrial College for Colored Persons (KSIC). The administration starts planning for four-year bachelor's degrees. Three female students die in Kentucky Hall fire.

1929   Hickman native Rufus B. Atwood begins his thirty-three-year tenure as president of Kentucky State.

1930   African Americans compose 8 percent of Kentucky's population.

        U.S. Census for Frankfort: 2,205 Blacks (18 percent) and 9,420 (82 percent) whites.

1933   The Grad Club is organized by Jackson K. Robb. Its original members were alumni of Mayo-Underwood and Clinton Street Schools. The club's original purpose was to support athletics at Mayo-Underwood High School. In the same year, the Women's Progressive Club is organized. Although it began as "just friends," the members felt a need for a recreational outlet and a venue for intellectual development.

1934   First of two national Negro College football championships (the second was in 1937) is earned by Kentucky State. The team is coached by Henry Arthur Kean, who studied under Knute Rockne during summers at Notre Dame.

1935   Charles Anderson Jr., a Frankfort native, is elected to the Kentucky General Assembly from Louisville's 42nd House District. Anderson attended Kentucky State and Wilberforce University and received his law degree from Howard University. He becomes the first Black legislator in the South since Reconstruction. His mother, Mrs. Anderson, was founder of Rosenwald PTA.

1937   Kentucky River flood affects South Frankfort and the "Craw/Bottom." Hundreds are displaced from their homes.

1938   On July 1, KSIC becomes Kentucky State College for Negroes. All collegiate-level courses taught at West Kentucky Industrial College are transferred to Kentucky State.

1940   African Americans compose 7.5 percent of Kentucky's population.

        U.S. Census for Frankfort: 1,680 Blacks (14 percent) and 9,812 (86 percent) whites.

1941　The U.S. enters World War II. Kentucky African Americans who serve in the armed forces during the war will number 20,220.

President Franklin D. Roosevelt issues an Executive Order that bans discrimination in defense industries, opening up many wartime jobs to Black citizens.

1942　Anna Mac Clarke, a 1941 graduate of Kentucky State, enlists in the Women's Army Corps. Clarke becomes the first Black woman to achieve the rank of an officer and command an all-white regiment.

1950　African Americans compose 7 percent of Kentucky's population.

U.S. Census for Frankfort: 1,492 Blacks (12 percent)and 10,424 (88 percent) whites.

The Kentucky General Assembly further amends the Day Law to permit Black students to enroll in integrated schools for courses not offered at Kentucky State College for Negroes.

1952　In anticipation of eventual desegregation, Kentucky State College drops "for Negroes" from its official name.

1955　Frankfort Independent Schools and Franklin County Schools begin the process of desegregation. Frankfort Board of Education proposes to transfer Black high-school students from Mayo-Underwood School to Frankfort High School.

1956　Kermit Williams is among the first Blacks to play football for the newly integrated Frankfort High School. In the September 17, 1956, issue of *Life Magazine,* a picture of Williams appears after he scored a touchdown. Behind him on the hill is a burning cross.

The first Black student to enroll at Elkhorn High School is George White Jr.

The first Black student to enroll at Bridgeport High School is William Joseph Stallard.

1959　Winnie A. Scott Hospital closes. King's Daughter's Memorial Hospital accepts patients without regard to race.

1960　African Americans compose 7.2 percent of Kentucky's population.

U.S. Census for Frankfort: 2,387 Blacks (11.5 percent) and 118,270 (88.4 percent) whites. Urban Renewal Agency creates a plan that eliminates many homes of Black residents in "the Bottom" area and forces many of them to relocate.

The legislature creates the Kentucky Commission on Human Rights and prohibits discrimination in state employment.

1960–61   Kentucky State faculty and students lead non-violent efforts to desegregate local restaurants, theatres, and other public accommodations.

1963   Governor Bert Combs issues executive order prohibiting racial segregation in public facilities. After protests, boycotts, and litigation, Frankfort's elementary schools are finally integrated.

Construction begins on Sutterlin Terrace public housing complex near Kentucky State.

1964   Historic March on Frankfort by local, state, and national Black leaders, including Dr. Martin Luther King Jr., emphasizes need to end racial discrimination in the state.

1966   The Kentucky General Assembly passes and Governor Edward T. Breathitt Jr. signs the first state civil rights act south of the Ohio River.

1967   Urban Renewal Agency purchases Corinthian Baptist Church property at 324 Mero Street for $60,000. Riverview Homes public housing units open near Capital Plaza office complex. First Corinthian Baptist Church dedicates new Education and Community Center Building at Second and Murray Streets.

1968   Black community and area adjacent to Kentucky State erupts in violence following murder of Dr. King.

1970   African Americans compose 7.2 percent of Kentucky's population.

U.S. Census for Frankfort: 2,647 (12 percent) Blacks and 18,653 (88 percent) whites.

1970–72   With players like Travis Grant and Elmore Smith, Kentucky State College wins three straight NAIA men's Division I basketball championships.

1972   Kentucky State College becomes Kentucky State University and offers a master's degree in public affairs.

1974   First Baptist Church and St. John A.M.E. Church are placed on the National Register of Historic Places. The Kentucky Historical Society erects historical markers in front of the churches.

1979   Contract is awarded on September 12, 1979, to construct a park for South Frankfort residents. It opens in June 1980.

1980   African Americans compose 7.1 percent of Kentucky's population.

U.S. Census for Frankfort: 3,362 (9 percent) Blacks and 35,810 (91 percent) whites.

1980   KSU wins the inaugural women's NAIA national basketball championship tournament.

1990   African Americans compose 7.1 percent of Kentucky's population.

        U.S. Census for Frankfort: 3,026 (10 percent) Blacks and 27,193 (90 percent) whites.

1991   Derrick Graham is the first Black elected to Frankfort City Council.

1992   The Center of Excellence for the Study of Kentucky African Americans [CESKAA] is established at Kentucky State University.

1993   Frankfort native George C. Wolfe wins a Tony Award for directing *Angels in America: Millennium*. He will go on to win another Tony for *Bring in 'da Noise/Bring in 'da Funk* and becomes producer of The Public Theatre/New York Shakespeare Festival.

1995   Maryland Avenue is renamed for Dr. Martin Luther King Jr.

1998   Historic marker is placed on former site of Mayo-Underwood School on Mero Street.

1999   Historic marker is placed on former site of Winnie A. Scott Hospital on 2nd Street.

2000   African Americans compose 7.3 percent of Kentucky's population

2002   Former City Commissioner Derrick Graham becomes the first Black elected state representative from the 57th House district, and Janice Wade is elected constable, becoming the first African American woman elected to office in Franklin County.

PHOTO CONTRIBUTORS

Lillian Barnett

Robert Basey

Bessie B. Bright

Cornelia F. Calhoun

Josephine Calhoun

Ora Mae Cheaney

Mary E. Clay

Bernice Combs

Nell Cox

Harry Craig

Mattie Davis

Ruby F. Dixon

Marjorie Doneghy

Mary E. Ellis

Helen C. Exum

Bill Feldman

Winona L. Fletcher

Gloria Giles

Henrietta Gill

Katie Johnson Graham

Grace T. Harris

Clara E. Hogan

Lucille Jameson

Billie Mack Johnson

Thomas Johnson

Dorothy G. Jones

Roberta Jennels Jones

Josephine W. Krank

Henry Mack

Andrew Mason Sr.

Kevin Mason

Sheila Mason Burton

Dorothy C. McGowan

Elizabeth McGrapth

George E. Mitchell

Rev. K. L. Moore

Mary J. Robinson

Anna J. Samuels

Mae and Alex Sanders

Ella Parker Sanders

Clarence Saunders

Margurite Shauntee

George Simmons

Archie L. Surratt

John Sykes

Edna Rawlings Washington

Mary Louise Jones Washington

William G. Washington

Carrie Watts

Barbara F. White

Evelyn Williams

Lillian Wright

ORAL HISTORY INTERVIEWS

Lillian Barnett, interview by Douglas A. Boyd, June 27, 2002.

Margaret Berry, interview by James E. Wallace, August 12, 1991.

Mary Helen Berry, interview by James E. Wallace, July 2, 1991.

James Calhoun, interview by James E. Wallace, July 16, 1991.

William Carl Calhoun, interview by Sheila Mason Burton, July 26, 1997.

James Preston Campbell, interview by Sheila Mason Burton, August 31, 1996.

Millie Combs, interview by Sheila Mason Burton, August 16, 1995.

Glen Douglas, interview by Sheila Mason Burton, August 31, 1996.

Henry and Margaret Ellis, interview by James E. Wallace, August 1, 1991.

James B. Ellis, interview by James E. Wallace, August 7, 1991.

Mary Emma Tracey Ellis, interview by James E. Wallace, October 5, 1992, and by Dr. Winona Fletcher, June 11, 1995.

William Isaac Fields, interview by James E. Wallace, May 15, 1991.

Henrietta Gill, interview by James E. Wallace, May 8, 1991.

James T. Graham, interview by James E. Wallace, May 21, 1991.

Clara E. Hogan, interview by Dr. Winona Fletcher, May 2, 1996.

Helen Holmes, interview by James E. Wallace, July 25, 1991.

Gladys Hutchison, interview by Doug Boyd, June 19, 2002.

Maggie Knott, interview by James E. Wallace, July 1, 1991.

Josephine Krank, interview by Dr. Winona Fletcher, June 3, 1996.

Henry P. Kemp, interview by Sheila Mason Burton, September 1, 1996.

Mary L. McGee, interview by Sheila Mason Burton, July 9, 1995.

Ellsworth Marshall Jr., interview by James E. Wallace, May 17, 1991.

Wesley "Joe" Marshall, interview by Sheila Mason Burton, September 12, 1995.

Margaret Barnett McIntosh, interview by Doug Boyd, June 27, 2002.

Rev. K.L. Moore, interview by Doug Boyd, June 6, 2002.

Alex Sanders, interview by James E. Wallace, March 27, 1991.

George Simmons and Henry Sanders, interview by James E. Wallace, May 29, 1991.

Margurite Shauntee, interview by Dr. Winona Fletcher, April 11, 1996.

Dr. Mary Smith, interview by Dr. Winona Fletcher, July 11, 1996.

Archie Surratt, interview by Dr. Winona Fletcher, March, 19, 1996.

John Sykes, interview by Doug Boyd, June 13, 2002.

William G. Washington, interview by Sheila Mason Burton, September 2, 1996.

Barbara White, interview by Doug Boyd, June 6, 2002.

Anna Belle Williams, interview by James E. Wallace, July 18, 1991.

Clarence Williams and Richard Williams, interview By Doug Boyd, June 4, 2002.

INDEX

The types used in this book,
Truesdell, Berkeley Oldstyle, and Goudy Old Style,
are based upon the designs of Frederic W. Goudy. Truesdell
was designed in 1930 and cut in 1931. ITC Berkeley Oldstyle,
issued in 1986, was designed by Tony Stan based on Goudy's
University of California Old Style completed in 1938 for
that institution and then made available to the public
by Lanston Monotype in 1959 as Californian.
Goudy Old Style dates from 1915.

Book design by Jonathan Greene;
text composition and photo layout by
Charles Chandler (The Typewright).

Printing and binding by
Thomson-Shore, Inc.